Life's a BITCH

and then

You Change Careers

Life's a BITCH *and then* You Change Careers

9 Steps to Get Out of Your Funk & On to Your Future

ANDREA KAY

STC PAPERBACKS | STEWART, TABORI & CHANG | NEW YORK

Published in 2005 by
Stewart, Tabori & Chang
An imprint of Harry N. Abrams, Inc.

Library of Congress Cataloging-in-Publication Data

Kay, Andrea
    Life's a bitch and then you change careers : 9 steps to
get out of your funk and on to your future / Andrea Kay
    p. cm.
    Includes index.
    ISBN 1-58479-487-9
    I. Career changes. II. Vocational guidance. III. Title.

HF5384.K393 2006
650.14—dc22   2005027658

Edited by Marisa Bulzone
Designed by Susi Oberhelman
Graphic Production by Kim Tyner

The text of this book was composed in Berthold Bodoni, New Caledonia and Folio.

Printed in the United States of America

10 9 8 7 6 5 4 3 2 1

First Printing

HNA
harry n. abrams, inc.
a subsidiary of La Martinière Groupe

115 West 18th Street
New York, NY 10011
www.hnabooks.com

Visit Andrea Kay at www.lifesabitchchangecareers.com

Contents

My Take on Changing Anything

Every spring and fall I run late because I never know what to wear. I spend too much time rummaging through my closet trying to piece together an outfit that in the spring doesn't look like winter anymore and reflects the new fashion; and in the fall doesn't look like summer and incorporates that season's style. At the end of the ordeal, clothes are strewn across the floor, bed and bathroom counter. It is a twice-a-year reminder of how much I really don't like change.

And yet, I always come around. I flip through the clothing catalogues and magazines. Eventually, I let go of my notion of last year's fashion that took me two months to embrace and in which I was comfortably entrenched by the end of the season. As I get a feel for what I might like that's new, I lug outdated skirts and too-wide-lapel jackets to the "other-closet pile" and tuck a few new items into my main closet. For five or so months, there is peace on earth. And then the process starts all over again.

In a year, change imposes itself in many other ways as well. This year, for example, I bought a new cell phone after seven years of clutching one that had lost its cover and the doohickey that keeps the battery intact (after I dropped the phone in parking lots several times.) There was also the new clock radio that I had to learn to program after accidentally tipping a glass of water into my old favorite that refused to wake me up any longer.

Then there are the friends who have died and whom I no longer have in my life to tell about my latest project and for them to eagerly ask, "How is it going?"

It's hardest to give up the people. I still have a pair of socks from junior high school that my grandfather gave me before he died when I was 15. And then there are the pets. I lost my dog and two cats to cancer in the last year and a half. I cling to their static photographs in the desperate hope to hold on.

In varying degrees, I grieve for anything that was and is no longer. You just get so used to the people, pets and things in your life being there. And even though you know nothing stays the same, there's a part of you that always hopes it will.

After working with people and their work issues for nearly 20 years, I have come to see that careers are also one of the hardest things for people to give up or begin anew. Work represents so much of a person—the place you can express yourself, learn about yourself and develop who you are. It's complicated.

Some people expect a lot from their work—maybe too much. Others don't want it to ever change. It is terribly inconvenient to have to start all over. Not to mention scary.

And if that weren't enough, when it comes to your career, there are two dynamics at war within you: the desire to be happy and the desire for security.

As you contemplate and make a career change, you might keep in the back of your mind my take on change. It is this: No matter how big or small the change, you are going to feel discomfort. It is to be expected. So let chaos reign. Don't try to avoid the discomfort. Metaphorically speaking, throw your clothes all over the floor, bed and bathroom counter. Then bring on the catalogues. There will always be new ones to thumb through—because nothing ever stays the same. That's a good thing if you want to continue to express yourself, learn about yourself and develop into who you are. Or perhaps more accurately, who you are becoming.

For Openers . . .

Life can be, well, a bitch when you're in the wrong career. I don't need to tell you how miserable it feels to spend your day in a place you don't want to be, doing work that your heart's not in. But I do need to tell you that it's possible to change. This book will show you how.

I know you've got good reasons for hesitating to take the leap. It's work to change careers, right? Who's got the time? You've got a family to support. You might have to start at the bottom and make less money. Besides, you don't know what else you'd do aside from what you're doing now.

But something has happened in your life to get you thinking seriously about making a career change this time. It's a good thing you're paying attention—because the last thing you want is to look back at your life and regret what you could have done but didn't.

Paying attention to your dissatisfaction and then taking the right steps to changing careers can change your life. When you create something that fits who you are, your life can be blissful, joyous, prosperous and meaningful—with you in control. Instead of counting the hours until each day ends, you will count your blessings that you get to do this work every day.

We'll take one step at a time to help you explore making a change and then be smart in doing it. This book isn't about just switching jobs or, as so many people say, finding "what's out there" or "having something to fall back on." It's about searching inside yourself and then searching for work that fits that self.

This can lead to a wise career change to make your life better. So this book is about how to create a career that fits your life and who you are.

To do that, I'm going to give you some very specific questions and exercises to complete along the way. You may not use every single piece of information you dig up. But following this structure is a process. And like most things, the process is the way by which you actually create the result you want. Although this process is systematic, it's also very organic. Sometimes events that take place or things you learn about yourself along the way create your path. You'll see how this happens as you meet people throughout the book and hear about the ways in which significant events or other discoveries have affected their thinking.

In the initial steps, we'll do some soul-searching, "blue-skying" and "what-iffing." Each step will build on the next. By carefully following each step, you will create your new, concrete career objective based on who you are—not who others think you should be.

Then we'll bring it back to earth and deal with other concerns, like *how* to make it happen. The worst thing you can do when making a career change is to start focusing on *how* you're going to make a change before you know where you're headed. It will only confuse you.

You will probably come up with some very cool ideas as you go through this process. A word of caution: You'll be tempted to start judging your ideas and thoughts as they come to you. That's natural but not smart.

In my first consultation with a 50-year-old teacher, she told me, "Someone suggested I become a travel agent. But I don't think that's realistic. I've always wanted to be around the outdoors, but I have no experience, so that's probably a stupid idea."

If you immediately focus on what's realistic or unrealistic and other reasons why you think you can't even explore an idea, you will get nowhere. So how shall I put this nicely—please keep your opinions

> *"I didn't have a very good reason for becoming a dentist. I was 13 or 14 and I liked my dentist. He was one of the few male influences in my life. My parents were divorced. He'd make a big fuss over me when he'd see me. He wore a white coat. It was prestigious."*
>
> MORRY, a dentist for 36 years

to yourself until we get to Step 8, OK? Then you can talk about everything that worries you.

Let's just imagine what *could be* for now. I promise, this book has a healthy mix of idealism and realism. You will need both to be successful in this process.

What's a Career Anyway?

Before we go further, let's focus briefly on what we're talking about here, and exactly what you're thinking about changing.

I define a career as a combination of:

- The particular occupation you choose to pursue and train for that is a significant part of your life and may or may not fit who you are
- The activities, experience, and knowledge you accumulate; skills you develop and progress you make while you're in that occupation

Let's say you choose to and are trained to be a physician. Throughout your career, you will have various jobs that comprise tasks and activities that physicians do. Early on, you might patch up people's injuries working in a hospital emergency room. Then you go into private practice, where you examine patients, analyze health issues and prescribe treatments. You could get a position as a physician for a corporation. Along the way, you take more classes and accumulate more knowledge. You might become a health care consultant to an insurance company. I know one physician who is a lexicographer—he edits medical dictionaries.

That's your potential career: a progression of particular roles and jobs physicians can do—all the while building your reputation, accumulating knowledge and fine-tuning your skills.

Many people—you might be one of them—don't put the kind of thought they need to into a choice of career. A *satisfying career* requires you to look inside yourself to know what type of work fits you. When the work doesn't fit who you are, you start thinking, "I need to make a career change."

What a career change means

Most people who claim they want to make a career change really don't mean it. Take the accountant who said, "I have to make a career change. I can't work in health care anymore. I'm thinking of going into manufacturing."

"Manufacturing?" I asked him. "What do you want to do there? Sell products, oversee operations or what?"

"No!" he exclaimed. "I want to be an accountant!"

As you can see, he didn't mean what he said when he declared he wanted to make a career change. He still wanted to do the things an accountant does, so it's not a career change. He just wanted to do it in a different industry. That's an industry change.

It's hard to get everyone to agree on the definition of a career change. Even the U.S. government throws up its hands and says, in so many words, "Beats us." The Bureau of Labor Statistics states on its Web site that it has never attempted to estimate the number of times people change careers in the course of their working lives because "no consensus has emerged on what constitutes a career change."

For example, the bureau cites the case of the Web-site designer who was laid off from a job, worked for six months for a lawn-care service and then found a new job as a Web-site designer.

"Might that example constitute two career changes?" the bureau asks. "If not, why not? Is spending six months at the lawn-care service long enough to consider that a career? How long must one stay in a particular line of work before it can be called a career?"

Time is not really the defining factor for a career. Some people work 20 years and never have a career. They have jobs. Bill, a 30-year-old unemployed worker who called me to say, "I need to make a career change," was one of those.

He'd had five jobs in eight years, including a sales role in a staffing service company, a customer service job in a financial services firm, a manager in a pizza place and a supervisor in a manufacturing plant. What he really needed was to get serious about figuring out what particular career he wanted to pursue—one that fit who he was and could be a significant and satisfying part of his life.

If you are someone like Bill, who is trying to figure out how to *start* his career, these nine steps are just what you need too.

So first let's define what a career change is.

My definition of career change is *conducting a search of yourself to move toward work that's more fitting to who you are.*

This means the work you will do:

- Uses your strengths
- Challenges you
- Is meaningful to you
- Fits your values and personality
- Fits into your life and the future you want to create

Your present or former career may or may not have used your strengths. You may have found it challenging and meaningful once—or never. It may have fit your life at one time.

But if you're going to make a career change now, you want to make one that incorporates these five things I just listed—as much as you can. They may not all be equally important to you and you may not get 100 percent of what you want. But these are the elements of a satisfying career.

This change may require new training. It may be related to the industry you're in now. For example, you might be a health care administrator who wants to be a nurse. Even though you're staying in the industry, you'll be making a career change because:

Your roles will be different.
A hospital administrator sets policies and procedures, oversees a staff that handles operational issues and works with the clinical staff of the hospital. A clinical nurse assists patients and doctors.

Your activities will vary.
As an administrator, you deal with day-to-day operational issues in your facility. You attend meetings with the community, staff or board members and develop budgets and interpret reports. As a nurse, you might be in the operating room or at patients' bedsides.

You'll have different experiences, use other knowledge and perhaps develop and use new skills.
As an administrator, you know about management principles and practices, budgets, cost containment, government regulations, giving

presentations and managing. Your key skills might be problem solving, planning, leading and communicating. As a nurse, your knowledge encompasses diseases and medical procedures and techniques, and your skills could include observing, reporting, collecting samples, performing laboratory tests, feeding, massage and applying dressings.

You'll progress differently and build a new reputation.
As an administrator, you may get a graduate degree, move to a larger facility or decide to take your expertise to a health insurance company. As a nurse, you may move to a doctor's office, surgical center, health care corporation or home health care service. You might add on management responsibilities or become a nurse-midwife or nurse anesthetist. I know of one nurse who runs her own tattoo removal company.

This is not to say that you will throw your former knowledge and skills out the window. You may end up utilizing many of the skills you used in your other career. Having been a hospital administrator, you have a lot of valuable experience and knowledge that will enhance your nursing career. Many skills are transferable to new careers. Although you are in the same industry, you are making a career change.

What's tugging at you to change?
Various things inspire people to make a career change:

A life event such as a divorce, turning 40 or 50, having a child, the completion of raising a family, becoming physically unable to do your present line of work or getting fired or laid off
Although some of these events aren't ones people choose, they can be a catalyst for something better. When Marie was "downsized" at her magazine, she said, "It was the best thing to happen to me in a long time. For months, there was a nagging suspicion that I should make a change, but I did not until I was forced. I knew in my heart I would bounce back and that this was meant to be."

As a result, Marie ended up creating a new career as a television producer, which she loves.

Linda had been in sales and marketing a good part of her career. But because of a movement disorder called cervical dystonia, she found it difficult to do her job, which required a lot of standing and moving around. She went on to create a new career for herself in which she consults with people who have experienced personal setbacks.

A woman I met at a writer's conference told me that she was changing careers because of how she felt after her father died. "It changed my whole outlook on life," she said. Instead of working in marketing for a company, she is pursuing a freelance writing career.

> "Since I changed careers, I hate to go to
> sleep and I can't wait to wake up in the morning."
>
> GARY DICK, owner of Gary's Classic Guitars

Retirement

A lot of retirees are looking at second careers. In fact, older workers—age 56 to 64—are predicted to make up 52 percent of the U.S. workforce by 2010 and those 65 and older are predicted to make up 30 percent of the workforce by 2010. Many will work in new careers. The AARP (formerly known as the American Association of Retired Persons) reports that 68 percent of workers age 50 to 70 expect to continue to work or never retire at all.

A 2005 study on aging and retirement conducted by Harris Interactive with HSBC and Age Wave showed that traditional retirement is a thing of the past. Among the more than 11,000 people interviewed worldwide, the study found that 80 percent want to scrap mandatory retirement and 75 percent want to keep working in their maturity.

William Safire is one of them. After writing more than 3,000 newspaper columns, Safire wrote his farewell column explaining why he was ending the column at age 75 and moving on to something else. He quoted two people who had given him advice about work.

Nobel Laureate James Watson told him, "Never retire. Your brain needs exercise or it will atrophy." And ad man Bruce Barton advised, "When you're through changing, you're through."

"Combine those two bits of counsel—never retire, but plan to change your career to keep your synapses snapping—and you can see the path I'm now taking," Safire wrote. He went on to explain that he's taking on the chairmanship of the Dana Foundation, a private philanthropic organization. "Retraining and fresh stimulation are what all of us should require in 'the last of life, for which the first was made.'"

The fact is that most work of the future will not require manual strength, but brain power instead. Many older workers wanting to stay mentally sharp and active may slow down and work fewer hours, but they will be more inclined to try new things that will offer more fulfillment in their next phase of life.

An unexpected experience that alters your course

Take Dr. Mark Rubin, who originally had been heading down the path to become an oceanographer when a bout of seasickness changed his plans. According to an article in *Dermatology Times*, he traveled to Nicaragua as a volunteer to help deliver a vaccination program to tiny villages. That's when Rubin decided to devote himself to people's medical needs. When he traveled to Thailand to work for the Ministry of Public Health in Bangkok, he was introduced to tropical medicine, which sparked his interest in diseases of the skin. As a result, he became a dermatologist.

Rabbi Edgar Weinsberg of Massachusetts also experienced an unexpected change. Due to a merger of synagogues, he had left his congregation of 21 years. So, at age 61, he decided to move to Florida to be close to his son and daughter-in-law and begin the process of finding a new role for himself.

Lost enthusiasm for your work—perhaps due to forces beyond your control

One of my clients had practiced industrial labor law for 20 years. But due to changes in the market and the geographic area where he lives, the practice was drying up. He was also disenchanted with the whole legal field and felt it was time for a change.

"I don't like all the increased pressure to produce more and more revenue every single year," he said. He also felt the law practice had changed from the past, "when it was a bit more civil and less cutthroat."

Troubled waters can be brewing in your industry or at your company. Another client had sold highly engineered motors for 15 years. He wasn't jumping for joy anyway, and when the manufacturer he worked for moved overseas, he saw the writing on the wall for the whole industry and decided it was a good time for a change.

When actor Peter Riegert came to my city to screen the first feature film he had directed, *King of the Corner*, he talked about what made him want to direct after 35 years of acting. "Survival," he said. "I needed to save my life." Although he's still acting and enjoys it (he stars in this film), he expressed the same longing of many career changers: The desire to be energized by doing something new.

A desire for more

You may want more quality of life, flexibility, freedom, challenge or meaning in your work. Some people feel burdened by their job. Others are bored. Some people are intent on getting somewhere, making something important happen or making something out of themselves. Many people just want to feel more in control. This usually comes down to having a career you enjoy and that allows you to have time for family or other interests. From these folks I often hear, "I want a life!"

A brush with death, a debilitating illness or physical ailment

Some professions are downright hard on the body. Even with no injuries, most ballet dancers quit between age 32 and 38. Other times, illness causes change. Diane hosted a show for the Home Shopping Network when she developed lupus and landed on disability. She returned to school, earned her doctorate at age 51 and became a psychologist. After Jim, a businessman in Georgia, had a massive heart attack and heart transplant, he decided he wanted to become an English teacher.

Leonard, a software analyst who sat in a cubicle all day, was 21 and weighed 310 pounds. "I woke up one day with swollen ankles and decided I had to do something about it."

But it doesn't have to come to that. Sometimes things just aren't clicking—or never did. A Gallup poll found that 55 percent of employees have no enthusiasm for their work. Fifty-four percent said they feel they are not utilizing their skills in their current job. Many people simply fall into their line of work and never take the time to explore who they are and find work that meshes with that.

Other people finally pay attention to something that's been tugging at them. They may not know exactly what they want to do next, but they know what they're doing now isn't it. They make up their mind to focus on how they can become exceptional rather than just focusing on survival. They decide to make a career choice for themselves instead of just for the paycheck.

Alan, a dissatisfied but financially successful sales representative in California, called me to figure out how to make a change. He said, "I've gotten the money part out of my system. I'm at a point where it's about my life now and not accumulating more stuff."

Another client, now deceased, worked as a dentist for 36 years. He told me, "Everything had become an effort. I just didn't have it in me to keep up with the technology of dentistry anymore. I had to do 42 hours of continuing education every two years. I'd sit in the classes for six to eight hours with everyone around me pontificating on drilling and new filling material. I'd be in the back of the room daydreaming and reading books on psychology. The nagging turned into pangs. I had to take pills to sleep and pills at the office to relax."

At 62, he sold his practice. He said, "It felt like a burden was lifted and I knew I never wanted to go back there again."

John, an information technology consultant, came to me at age 30. "I had just finished the business plan for my company," he said. "It was sitting next to my computer and I didn't want to do anything with it. My heart wasn't in it. In the back of my mind, I sensed that there was a better career path for me."

Another client who worked in marketing said he sat in his office, which had been converted from a janitor's closet, staring at the walls. "I was dying to work with people and help them somehow. I felt isolated and depressed. When I woke up every morning, I can honestly say life felt like a real bitch."

> *"Some people say they haven't yet found themselves. But the self is not something one finds; it is something one creates."*
>
> **THOMAS SZASZ**

Desire to change can happen at any age. I hear from plenty of 30-year-olds fretting about what they're doing with their life. For nearly 20 years, people of all ages have come to me for help to make a career change. But I have noticed that more people have considered a career change since September 11, 2001—a day that made them stop and examine their lives and realize that life is too short to spend in a career your heart is not in.

How serious are you?

Your next career probably won't come to you in a lightning bolt—although on television, for example, it can be depicted that way. On one episode of the television comedy show *George Lopez,* George's wife is lamenting that she always thought she'd have her own business and become a millionaire one day. So George builds her an office in their garage, equipped with a cubicle that houses a computer, phone and file cabinets. She is touched, but doesn't know what she'd do in her cubicle.

"Trust your gut," George says. But she hasn't a clue. Then she remembers that she forgot to cancel an order for something for a wedding she is planning. And—*voila!*—she exclaims, "That's it! I'll be a wedding planner! I love organizing and working with details." In less than one miraculous moment, she had figured out her new, fabulous career, in which she'll make gazillions of dollars and love every minute.

Fat chance of that happening. Most likely, you will need to commit to a step-by-step process to discover what you want and go after it. This will include soul-searching and research—a word many people cannot bring themselves to think about.

It is tempting to think that it would take less. I was giving a speech once and a man in the audience said, "There must be a way to just be able to figure out how to blend your life into a career you'd like. There just must be an easy way."

There is an expectation that every whim can be satisfied with the touch of a button and that you will find instant gratification with everything—including a new career. But if you are serious about changing your life, you will need to be tolerant of a process that requires patience.

So let's see how serious you are.

On a scale of 1 to 4, (with 1 meaning you strongly disagree and 4 meaning you strongly agree), rate the extent to which you agree or disagree with the following statements:

_____ If it's going to take more than 30 days to make this change, it could be a problem.

_____ I hate doing research and probably won't do it.

_____ If I have to think, forget it.

_____ If I have to use my imagination, forget it.

_____ If I have to think about my feelings, forget it.

_____ I do not want to go out and talk to people.

_____ It's hard for me to go against others' wishes and the status quo.

_____ I'm not very good at setting and keeping goals.

If you scored between 24 and 32, your commitment level is not there. You won't do a thorough, strategic job of exploring a career change. Odds are low that you will find a new career that is meaningful, fruitful and satisfying to you.

If you scored between 8 and 16, you're realistic about what it's going to take:

- A reasonable time line
- Research
- Introspection
- Imagination
- Input from other people
- Going against the grain of what others may think or what you've been told you "should" do
- Facing your fears
- Hard work
- Willingness to set a goal and stick with it faithfully

HOW MUCH DO YOU NEED TO KNOW TO BEGIN?

Do you know exactly what you want to do in your next career? Don't have a clue? It doesn't matter. What matters is that restlessness that's telling you to: 1) do something different—at least investigate it; 2) do that thing you *know* you want; or 3) figure out what you do want.

Throughout this book, I will give you tasks and suggest what you'll learn from a particular activity. Whether you should perform a certain activity and what you'll figure out from it will depend on whether you know what you want to do next, don't know or have some ideas. To understand how my references apply to you, it will be helpful to know where you stand at this moment. So, check the category that fits you best:

Which are you?

☐   I know exactly what I want to do next. (Crystal Clear)

☐   I don't have the slightest idea what I want to do next. (Clueless)

☐   I've got some ideas, but . . . (Fuzzy)

If you identified yourself as "Clueless," you are like the majority of people who tell me they don't know what they want to do next. This process will give you plenty of ideas and help you connect the dots.

If you identified yourself as "Fuzzy," this process helps you further clarify whether your ideas are a good fit. I once had a client who, after going through this process with me, decided that she was in the right field after all. She decided to remain a teacher.

If you're "Crystal Clear," the process is a good test to see if what you think you want is on the mark. It can also help you expand the ideas you now have about your next career and show you how to go about discovering your new career position.

THE BEAUTY OF MAKING THE RIGHT CHANGE

What could be finer than having a career in which:

- Your work feels important and meaningful
- You're challenged
- You feel like you're being yourself
- You're appreciated, rewarded and valued for your contribution
- There are a variety of things you like to do, and do well
- You have the flexibility to do your job in a way that fits your life and values
- You can see tangible results from the work you do

> F. Scott Fitzgerald said, "There are no second acts in American lives." He never met you.

This is what most people say they want in their career. Don't you? If you stop and say, I want to create that for myself—to one degree or another—and then do it, you will have a sense of control. You will feel committed to something you believe in. With that will come less stress, and you will be more likely to see things in your life as challenges instead of burdens.

Do you thirst for more? Do you wonder, "Is this all there is?" Are you tired of living a lie or biding your time until you can retire and have the life you want? Then my nine steps will help you create more meaning, more control and less stress in your life and work.

I am confident you have the creative energy and power to fan that spark inside you. In fact, as I heard Rabbi Norman Cohen of Minneapolis say at a dear friend's funeral, you have the obligation to tend to that spark in you and fan it into a flame that will light up your life and the lives of others.

Remember, you also have the freedom to choose. Many of us were taught at a very young age that the circumstances you find yourself in dominate your life and the direction you go in. But if you want to change the course of your life, you need to understand that even when you feel you have none, you always have a choice.

Ready to begin?

Step 1

Discover that restless gnawing in the pit of your gut.

f I were a betting person, I'd say there is a restless gnawing in the pit of your gut that bothers you regularly, if not daily. It's a kind of nudge that has been there for some time. And in its quiet way, it beckons you—no, *bugs* you—to notice that something better awaits you.

You may have tried to ignore it, laugh it off or dismiss it. But the throbbing is there for good reason. It's a symptom of something that needs to be addressed. It's a warning sign, like the squeezing pain that some people get in the center of their chest to alert them that something is wrong with their heart.

In this case, the restless ache is commanding, "Look inside! There's more to you! And I will prey on your mind and haunt your dreams until you pay attention!"

This gnawing might be an idea that has drifted in and out of your head for years. Or a thought you get when you daydream or sit in boring meetings and fantasize about what you'd *really* like to be doing. It's a feeling that hits you when you let your mind wander. Or perhaps it's a voice that keeps coming around again and again, nagging at you.

If you're like a lot of people, though, you may sense the gnawing but aren't sure what it means or what to call it. Or what you should do about it. Or if what you *think* you should do about it will work.

You'll never know what you can achieve if you don't take the first step: starting to peer at what is in you. Your gut is the first place to look.

A man in Florham Park, New Jersey, once asked me, "I know there are no guarantees in life, but how does someone ensure they won't spend their twilight years saying, 'Wish I had'?" I suggested he

"*As soon as you trust yourself, you will know how to live.*"

GOETHE

WHAT DO YOU KNOW ABOUT YOURSELF THAT NOBODY ELSE DOES?

In an interview on the television program *60 Minutes* in 2004, singer-songwriter Bob Dylan described what that restless gnawing feels like. He told correspondent Ed Bradley, "I always knew that there was something out there that I needed to get to." Even at age 19, he believed he was destined to become a music legend.

"I was heading for the fantastic lights. Destiny was looking right at me and nobody else," he wrote in his memoir, *Chronicles, Volume One*.

When Bradley asked him what *destiny* meant to him, he replied: "It's a feeling you have that you know something about yourself nobody else does . . ."

pay attention to that thing he wished for—that restless gnawing in the pit of his gut. Put simply, it is the sense that he is meant to do more.

And that is *your* first assignment in this process—to give that "longing for something more" feeling your full attention.

Start by writing down observations and thoughts on what you have always been attracted to. For example, Beth Ann told me that since junior high she has picked up and bought psychology books at used-book stores. She said, "I always wondered what made people tick and relationships work. I was attracted to these books."

As long as Phillip can remember, he has been creating dinner parties with themes and planning and creating special events for his family and the professional organizations he's belonged to. He can do everything, from coming up with party favors, table settings, food and entertainment to overseeing the logistics and invitations.

Look at what you're drawn to. What section of the bookstore do you gravitate toward? Do you have a hobby you've been thinking about turning into your next career?

Write down what is summoning you—no matter how vague or specific it is at this moment. Put down what you know is true. You can't prove it, you just know it. It could be something you've never told anyone or thought wasn't possible. Yet, it's lingered in your mind forever.

Here are some examples of how other people have described their gnawing or what they just knew to be true about themselves:

- It would be great if I could help young people to love to learn.
- I don't know what to call it, but I really want to improve the health and well-being of people.
- I'm a frustrated explorer.
- I was born to do great things.*
- In the back of my mind, I sense there is a path that better uses my personal strengths, and one that is more personally rewarding.
- I want to be around art all the time. Not necessarily making it, but being a part of it.
- I want to be able to create memorable experiences for people by doing something with food.
- I love the environment. I want to help people appreciate and take responsibility for it.
- I always wanted to be involved in movies, but I don't know how.
- I want to sing!
- I felt writing was my destiny.
- I've always dreamed of working in film and am a movie fanatic. I've also loved listening to NPR and dreamed of being on it.
- I wanted to understand what made people unhappy and then help them understand how they could feel more like themselves and have a more meaningful and content life.
- I'm intrigued by digital technology and devices that look cool and that people can use.
- I always envision space and how to configure objects with color and materials in a space.

- I want to help people solve their personal problems so they can have better lives.
- I want to improve the lives of animals.
- It haunts me; it won't leave me alone—to do something with water sailing.
- I have chosen to recycle scrap metal to create my art forms; to recycle is to take special care of our resources, ourselves, the future of our children and our planet.
- I always found human behavior interesting and I watch and analyze people at restaurants and make up stories. Being a therapist nags at me.
- I sense I need to develop a path for myself. Staring at a computer doesn't feel right.
- Intuition tells me I am on this earth to create art.**
- I want to live more simply the rest of my life.***

Put what gnaws at you into your own words. This doesn't have to be a statement of what you'll do or what your next career is called. Far from it. The exception to that is if you have already identified yourself as "Crystal Clear" and you can say with certainty, "I want to be a therapist" or "I want to sing!" If that's the case, then that's how you'll describe your restlessness. If you're "Fuzzy" or "Clueless," look at the following exercise as your first stab at peering at that spark that's inside you and dying to be lit—just one part of the puzzle.

> *"Knock on the sky and listen to the sound."*
>
> ZEN SAYING

---

*Oprah Winfrey said this in an interview with Barbara Walters. **Columbian-born artist Francisco Sanabria wrote this on the back of one of his pieces of art. ***From Laura Jackson, whom I read about in an Associated Press article. She gave up her career as a documentary filmmaker to learn how to become a farmer.

> *"I've been training myself to do open-water sailing and get certifications. It haunts me. I'm acutely aware of it all the time. It won't leave me alone."*
>
> **ALEX,** sales representative

Exercise: Getting at That Restless Gnawing

HERE'S WHAT YOU'LL NEED:

1. A cup of relaxing tea (see recipes on pages 32–33)
2. A pencil with a good eraser
3. This book—open to this page
4. A quiet place—a room at home or outside where you can hear the sound of your own breathing and nothing else (chirping birds are OK)

HERE'S WHAT YOU DO:

1. Take your tea, pencil and book to the place where you won't be interrupted.
2. Get comfortable and settled.
3. Close your eyes, take a deep breath, let it out; take another deep breath and let it out. Relax.
4. Now let yourself peer inside your heart and mind at that dream you are guarding within yourself. Ask:

- What is that restless gnawing saying?
- What is it nudging me to check out?
- What is it bidding me to do?
- What yearns to be expressed?
- What have I been wondering about for years?
- What do I simply know to be true about myself?

Don't do anything with it. Don't judge whether it's stupid, doable or not, too vague or too specific. Don't think about how or if you'll get there. Just let whatever you wrote sit on this page. And when you leave this quiet place and go back to your life, let the thoughts you wrote down swim around in your head. Give them time to percolate.

Keep them in the back of your mind as you go through the rest of these steps. What you come up with here might be the one ingredient, idea or glue that binds together everything else you learn about yourself. Just let it become part of what you ponder as you continue.

You've just completed the first step, taking that longing to a new level—a level you had to go to. Because the gnawing will keep trying to get your attention until you give it yours.

Relaxing Tea Recipes

Use these for the previous exercise.

LILY'S GARDEN RELAXATION TEA

From Kim Falcone, herbalist, Lily's Garden, Wakefield, Rhode Island. Kim said these herbs are usually available at any natural-foods grocery or health-food store that has a bulk-herb section, or through an herbal apothecary. Herb shops will be more likely to carry the milky oats. She said they are safe to take with other medicines and pharmaceutical drugs.

2 parts milky oat tops
2 parts chamomile flowers
2 parts lavender flowers
1 part spearmint leaves

Mix herbs together. Pour 8 ounces of boiling water over one heaping teaspoon of herbs. Cover and let steep 20 minutes. Strain off herbs and enjoy!

7 TIPS FOR SUCCEEDING IN A CAREER CHANGE

1. Think through the pros of making your career change so you can see how they outweigh the cons

2. Understand that you're committing to work hard at this

3. Have confidence in your ability to make the change

4. Set realistic goals

5. Develop a plan

6. Track your progress

7. Reward yourself along the way

The following recipes are from Dr. Michael Wayne, practitioner of Chinese medicine and author of *Quantum-Integral Medicine: Towards a New Science of Healing and Human Potential*. Most likely, you will find these herbs at an herbal apothecary. Dr. Wayne said both teas are safe to take with other medicines or drugs.

HAPPY TEA

9 grams each licorice and wheat
10 pieces jujube fruit
9 grams each cinnamon twigs and salvia root

Place all ingredients in a pot with 5 cups of water, bring to a boil and simmer for a half hour.

RELAXED WANDERER

9 grams each bupleurum, dang gui, white peony, astragalus
    and schizandra
5 grams licorice

Place all ingredients in a pot with 5 cups of water, bring to a boil and simmer for a half hour.

Step 2

Track down the bugs.

Here is your chance to get everything that's bugging you about your career off your chest, and to accomplish three other things:

1. Gain a better understanding of what hasn't worked in your career, which will help you better formulate what you *do* want
2. Avoid repeating mistakes and choosing more work that's not in your best interest
3. Discover language to help explain—when the time comes—why you want to change careers

So get out a pencil or pen, because you're going to think through and write answers to questions that will tell you:

1. Why you want to change careers
2. What specifically hasn't been right about your career
3. How your career up to now has adversely affected your life

Up to now, you've probably been too busy to actually sit down and write this. Or you've never been encouraged to reflect on it. But you're doomed to repeat the past if you don't go through this part of the process. It also can feel good to complain to somebody. So lay it on me.

> *"I got tired of spending years defending strategies I knew were flawed, of working with values that weren't my own, of being responsible to chief executives and boards that were under huge pressure to perform."*
>
> **A CHIEF FINANCIAL OFFICER**
> who runs a sporting-goods business in Massachusetts,
> featured in a 2004 *New York Times* article

It's not that we're going to dwell on what's not working now or hasn't been right in the past—or worry about how you got here. But to help move toward a better future, you need to put on the table what's not cutting it. When we get to Step 9, on marketing yourself, some of this information—in edited form—will come in handy in formulating your rationale for making a move.

In addition, you might be like some people for whom talking about or seeing what is wrong helps them solve a piece of the puzzle. This can give you a clearer picture of what you want. Joel, an actor, is a good example. Although he loved acting, it is a tough business to succeed in, and he found himself in odd jobs more often than doing the thing he loved. Much of the time he worked as a bartender:

> *"My job was to serve drinks. I was dependent on tips from customers. However, I saw so many people abusing the alcohol that it put me in a tough situation. If I cut them off, I'd get small tips; if I let them drink, my conscience couldn't handle the possibility that these people would hurt someone or themselves. Consequently, I made very little money and pissed people off. It made me realize that deep down I wanted to help people."*

Will, who had been a renovation contractor, enjoyed his work but it took its toll, both mentally and physically:

> *"I was creating things. There was a real sense of satisfaction in transforming something into something else. I liked the permanence of it, and people would be happy at the end with what you did. But I didn't like the physicality of the work. And it didn't appeal to me intellectually. I wanted to use my intellect instead of my body to transform things."*

Let's start this step by answering the following questions:

1. What is prompting you to want to make a career change?
In one sentence, explain what's going on in your life that has brought you to this point:

_____

_____

_____

_____

_____

_____

_____

_____

_____

_____

_____

_____

_____

_____

EXAMPLES OF WHAT OTHERS SAY:

"I'm a 52-year-old dentist who can't physically do this work anymore."
"I'm a 48-year-old executive who can retire early and now do what I want."
"I'm a 32-year-old programmer who hates being a programmer."
"I don't believe in what I'm doing anymore."
"I'm a 38-year-old sales consultant who always wanted to sing."
"I've been a stay-at-home mom and returning to a career I want to enjoy this time."
"I'm a retiring teacher but I'm not ready to stop working. Now I want to do something that gives me more time for myself and is less stressful."

Life was a bitch for Charlie, a police officer in Camden, New Jersey, for 23 years.

"The career of a street cop is one filled with boredom or the terror of a robbery in progress, rapist on the loose or a murder that just took place. It was a job where you prayed you would make it home some nights to go to an officer's funeral the next day," he said.

When he decided to make a change, he said, "I was beat up and tired, exhausted physically, emotionally and spiritually."

"I was a 40-year-old studio executive who hadn't produced a movie and was out of work again in a business that relentlessly craves the youth culture."

"I don't have the personality to do the relentless selling."

"I was laid off after 15 years at my company. It's time to have a career that fits who I am and is more meaningful."

"I've spent a lot of time not seeing what's around me. I don't want to spend the rest of my life like that."

"I've taught middle-school English for two years and already feel burned out."

"I was a 46-year-old actor, but much of the time I was waiting tables and doing other work which was not very fulfilling."

"I am spending 50 percent of my time resolving problems instead of doing the fun part of being an interior designer. It's not personally or financially rewarding anymore."

"My work feels superficial. I want to have a deeper impact on people's lives."

"I felt as if I were on an assembly line, churning out story after story, day after day in the newspaper business—which is all-consuming and often difficult to have a life after work."

"I don't want to just manage day-to-day operations. I want to create something new."

"I spent the first half of my career in business. I want the second half to be more creative."

2. What do (or did) you dislike about your present or past jobs?
Specifically, what are you (or were you) *doing* daily that you dislike?
Think through the jobs you've had. What specific *function* or *functions*
have you *not* enjoyed? Describe the action you were performing that
you disliked:

_____

_____

_____

_____

_____

_____

_____

_____

_____

_____

_____

EXAMPLES:

> Dealing with customers
> Writing a weekly newsletter and being on constant deadlines
> Writing reports and presenting them to management
> Answering phones, filing and secretarial work
> Creating budgets
> Managing teams
> Organizing events
> Managing the daily operations of an office
> Editing documents
> Training employees
> Fixing problems with orders and other things that went wrong

3. What do (or did) you dislike about the environment you work in?

_____

_____

_____

_____

_____

_____

_____

_____

_____

EXAMPLES:

> It was very structured. I had to report in a lot. I'm used to
> working on my own.
> The hours were inflexible. I couldn't work from home.
> The place was too hierarchical and formal.
> The company was close-minded.
> I had to work in a lab.
> I was in an office and never outside, where I need to be.

> *"I was 'too nice' to be in newspaper work. I was
> tired of being forced to be sarcastic when I didn't want
> to be. I wanted to be on the inside instead of
> always being a reporter on the outside looking in and
> never being able to participate."*
>
> MARIE, newspaper and magazine reporter for 20 years

ANOTHER REASON TO CHANGE: BOREDOM CAN KILL YOU

You can become "literally bored to death, because long-term boredom has the same impact on the body as stress," said Martyn Dyer-Smith, psychologist at Northumbria University in England, in the *Daily Record*. It can lead to heart trouble and suppression of the immune system.

"Boredom causes raised blood pressure, narrowing of the arteries and raised cholesterol," said Dr. Sandi Mann, author of *Hiding What We Feel, Faking What We Don't*.

If you find yourself tired, drained, sick a lot, irritable and easily distracted, boredom may be affecting your health and you need to examine the work you're doing. Keep in mind that not every single moment is going to be stimulating. It's the long periods of boredom you need to watch out for.

As Lewis Carroll wrote in *Alice in Wonderland*, "If you drink too much from a bottle marked 'poison,' it's almost certain to disagree with you sooner or later."

4. Describe the culture of the organization that you work for (or worked for) that you don't like:

_____

_____

_____

_____

_____

_____

_____

Managers don't give feedback or communicate.

All they care about is making money.

The company is not community oriented.

They don't care about balance and the fact that people
    have personal lives.

Employees were a number.

Management wasn't supportive.

5. What do you never want to do again?

_____

_____

_____

_____

_____

_____

_____

_____

_____

_____

EXAMPLES:

Meet a monthly quota

Sit by myself in a room all day

Direct, cold-call sales

Travel

Diagnose mechanical problems

Support information systems and applications

Keep time sheets

Work with children

Be fearful for my life

Be bored

6. How has being in this work affected your life overall? In other words, how is life a bitch?

EXAMPLES:

I am exhausted all the time.

I am emotionally drained and have no time for my family.

I feel like my talents are going to waste.

I'm depressed and unmotivated.

I have no life other than work.

I live in fear of not making anything of my life.

All I do is complain to everyone around me.

My blood pressure is sky high, and I am chronically stressed.

Life had become intolerable for Phillip, a lawyer with more than 15 years of experience, because the values of his industry had changed a great deal and no longer meshed with his.

"I took a very hard look at the profession, and I think lawyers are responsible for many problems in society, such as people not accepting responsibility for their own problems and the skyrocketing costs of doing business and insurance premiums, as well as medical insurance and costs," he said.

The Gist of Why You Want to Change Careers

Putting together all of the information you just wrote, clearly and concisely summarize *why* you want to change careers:

_____

_____

_____

_____

_____

_____

_____

_____

_____

_____

_____

_____

_____

_____

_____

EXAMPLE:

"I'm a 38-year-old sales consultant who hates the pressure of monthly quotas, bugging people to buy something and working for an organization that only cares about making money. As a result, I'm under considerable stress."

Keep this information tucked away for future reference.

Now let's look at what you have enjoyed doing in your life and work up until now.

Step 3

Pinpoint the good.

ow that we're done dredging up what hasn't been so great, let's look at what does work well. We're going to take a deeper look at you and identify what you have enjoyed doing and why—today or in past careers and jobs and in life in general. This will help shed light on what's been good so you can:

1. Build on that and possibly leverage it into a new career
2. Better formulate what you want to do next
3. Get clearer on what you enjoy doing most to make it the basis for your next career

This is really important: to be able to articulate what you like to do by describing basic, concrete skills. Because the foundation for this search of a new career isn't about what you want to *be*. It's based on what you can and love to *do*.

I'll tell you right here, though, it's hard to describe what you like to actually *do*. When I ask most people what they like to do and what their greatest strengths are, they can list two, maybe three, things.

"I'm good with people," they'll start with. "I'm good at analyzing. You can always count on me. And I always get the job done," they'll say.

"But what are you *doing* when you're getting the job done?" I ask.

"I'm doing it. The job," they say.

That could be anything. Writing, pushing, fixing, monitoring, researching, leading, problem solving, drawing, computing or observing something. *Reflecting on* and *writing about* what you actually do take more thought.

> "What lies behind us and what lies before us are small matters compared to what lies within us."
>
> RALPH WALDO EMERSON

WHY TESTS DON'T TELL YOU WHAT YOU SHOULD DO

WHAT VARIOUS TESTS DO:

▷ Ask you to pick occupations that sound good or ask how you'd behave in a particular situation, so that you can get data about your personality type and how well-suited you might be for a particular career

▷ Stimulate awareness about yourself and ideas by offering possibilities that might match with your skills and interests

▷ Identify and categorize your temperament and tendencies in comparison with other people

▷ Measure your interests, skills or values

TESTS DON'T:

▷ Predict what career you should be in based on your personality

▷ Tell you how well you'll handle a certain job

▷ Tell you the whole truth and nothing but the truth about who you are

▷ Tell you what's unique about you

▷ Show you the whole picture, since a satisfying career is much more than your personality and skills

▷ Necessarily offer accurate or reliable information—especially when you're answering questions about how you'd behave

▷ Usually tell you more about yourself than you already knew

USE TESTS TO:

▷ Generate ideas

▷ Supplement other information you gain from self-examination and research

▷ Possibly offer insight into whatever you're trying to discover about yourself

> *"I don't paint to live, I live to paint."*
>
> American artist **WILLEM DE KOONING**, who died in April 1997 at age 92

How do you get at this information? By writing answers to the following questions, which focus on what you like about where you are now or have been in the past. Specifically:

1. What are you doing now (or were you doing) daily in your work that you do well and enjoy?

Think through the jobs you've had. You may not like your job overall, but what specific function or functions have you enjoyed? Don't write things like "Revenue and market share growth." This is not something you do. Write simple verbs that describe the action you were performing and enjoyed. Break down what you do into basic functions. Add a subject if it's relevant or if you need to be more specific.

_____

_____

_____

_____

_____

_____

_____

_____

_____

_____

_____

_____

_____

Write
Coach others
Help people to perform physical tasks
Analyze something (data, computer models, behavior, figures)
Teach nontechnical people technical concepts (or something else)
Research
Persuade someone to take an action
Lead teams
Advise
Systematize information
Communicate
Cultivate relationships with others
Act as a liaison between management and customers or others
Visualize functional space and configuration of objects
Draw
Monitor
Solve problems
Conceive
Organize meetings and events
Plan projects from beginning to end

"Doing these steps, I realized my skills are transferable. Managing projects, organizing and communicating are skills I nurtured in my former career at my old company. Now I'm having fun organizing, managing projects and talking to people—doing all the things I figured out I enjoy doing, but in a different way and in a different environment."

BETH, former engineer turned entrepreneur

2. What were you doing in a project outside of work that you enjoyed and did well?

These could be times you've volunteered or participated in events that weren't necessarily part of your job. Again, write specific *verbs* that describe the action you performed and enjoyed.

_____

_____

_____

_____

_____

_____

_____

_____

Phillip, my client who has been a lawyer for more than 20 years, told me about the dozens of special events, conventions and parties he had planned for his professional associations and church:

> *"I handled all the logistics—I booked the hotel accommodations and convention facilities, planned the banquet menus and dealt with catering, coordinated registration and promotion, came up with themes, booked entertainment, found the speakers and organized recreation."*

Some of the skills he used to do this were *planning, organizing, coordinating, communicating, following up on details, creating, monitoring, researching* and *negotiating.*

Joel, the stage actor, told me:

> *"In many of the shows I did I would be the resident 'doctor,' suggesting herbal remedies to other actors."*

Some of the skills he used to do this were *evaluating, communicating* and *analyzing.*

Give presentations to an audience
Act as a mentor
Assist people in performing physical tasks
Teach
Persuade someone to do something
Follow up on details
Research information
Promote something
Plan and organize an event
Create or coordinate something (entertainment,
    speakers, meetings)
Prepare food

3. What would you like to continue to do more of? Look at your lists from the preceding questions.

_____

_____

_____

_____

_____

_____

YOU ARE NOT A JOB TITLE

It's natural to want to call yourself something.

But to explore what you want to do next, you need to see yourself

as a walking, talking body of skills instead of a job title.

4. Make a master list of all the skills you said you enjoyed using in these situations.

Now prioritize them. Out of everything on the list, what do you enjoy the most, second most, third and so on?

_____

_____

_____

_____

_____

_____

_____

_____

Write the skills that you numbered 1 through 6. From now on, we'll refer to these as your most joyful skills:

_____

_____

_____

_____

_____

_____

_____

_____

_____

_____

Summarize what you've enjoyed doing most and do well

Using your most joyful skills you just wrote down, along with any other descriptions, clearly and concisely summarize the functions you have enjoyed doing most in your career or life experiences.

_____

_____

_____

_____

_____

_____

_____

_____

_____

_____

EXAMPLE:
I have enjoyed coaching and advising people, training, writing, planning projects from beginning to end and researching information.

A new you

Starting now, begin to see yourself as this body of walking, talking skills that you carry around with you. You can use these skills in different situations and ways. They are always there inside you and ready to be offered up.

Let's say, for example, you are an engineer and you *design* aircraft engines. You also *analyze* and *research* data and performance. Part of your job is to *create* engine models and *evaluate* capabilities to

WHY WOULD A SUCCESSFUL EXECUTIVE GIVE IT ALL UP TO SELL GUITARS?

Gary Dick had a full-time job as a national sales account manager for a telecommunications company. He enjoyed it. He made good money. But at 41, he gave up his day job to collect and sell high-end and collectible twentieth-century guitars, mandolins and banjos, opening Gary's Classic Guitars on a full-time basis. Why would he take such a risk?

It started when Gary was 11 years old. His parents rented a guitar and an amplifier, and he took his first guitar lesson. Then, at 13, his cousin took him to a Beach Boys concert and the roots of his dream career took hold.

"When I saw them on stage with their guitars—the shape, the colors—I almost flipped out, seeing Fender Stratocaster guitars—the kind played by Jimi Hendrix and Eric Clapton," says Gary. "I took all my Bar Mitzvah checks and went to the music store, turned in my rented guitar and bought one of those and a matching amplifier. In 1965 it cost $529."

He didn't stop there. "I was always questing for something better. I was taken by a band called The Ventures, so now I had to have a Mosrite Mark I Ventures guitar. I had to sell my beloved Stratocaster and borrow $85 from my dad."

He continued to buy other guitars with money he made from various jobs, and in college he discovered a company in New York that buys and sells guitars and mandolins.

"I sold a vintage guitar to them for what at that time I'd call a windfall. I knew how to find guitars, primarily from the 1940s, 1950s and 1960s, in trader magazines and through word of mouth. What I didn't realize then was that I had a gift for this and there was a market for it."

Until 1980, trading and selling vintage guitars was a hobby in which Gary made a little money and slowly upgraded his collection. But then, as he put it, "Something big happened."

"I heard there were guitar shows where other enthusiasts like me were meeting in Dallas, Texas, and they were going to display these guitars. I went down there. There were about 40 guitars—a room full of everything I loved. I was breathless.

"I lived for these shows, which were only once a year. It was infectious. I could see the possibilities for money to be made in buying, selling and trading. It was clear as a bell."

Guitar trading magazines began to spring up and "people from around the world were coming to these shows—Japanese, Germans, Swiss, French. The market exploded. I had a knack for developing relationships and a lot of them became customers."

"It got to the point I had so much activity going on with the guitar business, my body was at my day job but my mind was back at home with the guitars. I talked to dozens of people in the field to try to define my own little slice of the pie. I had a lot of family responsibilities and the risk was high. No one could be sure this growing interest in rare and collectible guitars was sustainable. With the encouragement of friends and family over two years, I made the change."

In less than a year, his business was doing well. Today his customers include bankers, lawyers, not-so-famous musicians and some well-known people, including Jay Leno and Peter Frampton.

demonstrate product feasibility. You *communicate* with management and customers to determine their needs and participate on teams to evaluate product design.

You may not want to design aircraft engines anymore. But look at the various skills you use, probably enjoy and have honed: the ability to design, analyze, create, evaluate and communicate. These are distinct, functional skills that you can pick up, pack up and use in a new situation with different people and in different ways—or not. You don't *have* to use them all. You may not enjoy doing *all* of these things.

One of my clients, Jerry, had worked in a university bookstore, where he had a dual role as an operations analyst and sales associate.

His favorite part of this work was when he *assessed* customers' needs for computer hardware and software; *consulted* with students and professors; *researched* hardware and software compatibility, performance and price; and *created* an e-commerce Web site and the graphics for promotions.

He enjoyed all of those functions and wanted to continue using those skills. He just didn't want to consult, research, assess and counsel students and professors on computers anymore. His skills didn't shrivel up and go to waste—they were still very much a part of him. But he didn't know that until we actually identified his most joyful skills and he was able to see how he had used them so effectively in the past.

Beth Ann was an interior designer for 17 years. She loved using her visual skills, developing rapport with clients, being able to "pull out of people who they were" and articulate their needs and resolve conflicts, for example, between a couple who wanted two different looks. But, she said, "Even though I loved the design work, I wanted to have a deeper impact on people's lives."

Her skills didn't go away either. I'm jumping ahead here, but eventually she did find a very rewarding way to contribute her most joyful skills. She began a new career working with individuals, couples and families as a mental health counselor.

My client who had been a teacher for 30 years loved writing lesson plans, presenting ideas and helping others learn new concepts. She just didn't want to do that with kids anymore. She is exploring how she can enrich the lives of adults by using her strengths to create interesting curricula, give insight into a subject, clearly communicate concepts and coordinate field trips.

So, look at the functional skills you identified as your six most joyful skills and think of them as things that you have done well and enjoyed in the past, and can do in new environments and situations in your future. This is a fundamental piece of your new career.

Now that you can more clearly see what you like to do most, if you haven't been using these most enjoyable skills, you may be saying, "No wonder I haven't been happy in my work."

Step 4

Name who you like most and where you want to hang out.

N ow that you have an idea of what you enjoy *doing* most by defining your six most joyful skills, let's look at several other important aspects:

1. Who you might enjoy using those skills with
2. In what types of situations and environments you would like to use them
3. What else is tucked away in that heart and mind of yours that will be useful in figuring out your next career

This is going to help you further describe what might be possible and what your ideal situation could look like or be. Notice I said *could*. You don't know yet what's possible.

Look back at what you identified as your six most joyful skills. Remember, these are things that you have done well and enjoyed in the past, and can do in new environments and situations in your future. This is a fundamental piece to your new career.

Write those six most joyful skills you identified at the end of Step 3 here:

_____

_____

_____

_____

_____

_____

_____

_____

_____

_____

Now answer these questions:

1. Is there someone or a certain group or type of person you want to use these most joyful skills with?

To help you think about this, look at who you were working with when you enjoyed the activities at work or elsewhere that you described in Step 3. Were you using these skills with clients? If so, what kind? Were you working with adults, children, executives, artists, scientists or parents?

If you liked using the skills but not the people you were using them with, what type of person *would* you like to use them with? Is this person in the business world or are they a consumer? Or is there another type you've always wanted to work with? Animals? The handicapped? Elderly? Executives? People in pain? Families who need help?

When my client, Jerry, the bookstore operations analyst and sales associate, told me what he had enjoyed doing most outside of his work (but had never been paid for), it was *assessing* and *advising* his friends on how to develop good eating habits, exercise programs and healthier lifestyles, and coming up with eating plans and exercise regimens for them.

Remember, he enjoyed *doing* the same thing at his paid job—*assessing, advising, consulting,* and *counseling.* So in thinking about *who* he might want to work with next and apply these most joyful skills, he liked the idea of working with people who are dissatisfied with their weight and health. We didn't know what he was going to *do* with these folks yet—just that he liked working with that category of individuals. And as you'll see later, knowing that helped him define what he would end up doing in his new career.

My retiring-teacher client, who had been around 12- and 13-year-olds for 30 years, knew she now wanted to work with adults who were eager to learn, so that is how she answered the question.

Sometimes people tell me they know they want to help other people in some way, to which I always ask, "What kinds of people?"

My client Lisa defined her favorite people as, "People who need information that will simplify their lives." As we explored this further, she defined it more, saying, "Parents who need help finding the right schools for their special-needs children. Elderly people who need health care."

Write here what types of people or group you might like to use your most joyful skills with:

_____

_____

_____

_____

_____

_____

_____

_____

_____

_____

ENVIRONMENTS SHIFT WITH INDIVIDUAL VALUES

Many workers in the software world are working less punishing hours, according to an article on CNETNews.com. This might be because programmers have been putting greater emphasis on life outside work, while others say software houses have learned to manage projects better. The industry has realized that "productivity suffers when employees work extended days month after month."

But in the fast-growing computer-game industry, long hours continue to be commonplace. "A tough-guy culture among coders" seems to be a factor in what the International Game Developers Association calls "horrible working conditions in the computer-game world."

2. What have you liked about the environments you've worked in?

If you've never liked an environment, describe what you *would* like. Another way to look at this is to think about what kinds of situations you thrive in.

Write here what you liked about the environments you've worked in and thrived in or what you would like:

_____

_____

_____

_____

_____

_____

_____

_____

_____

_____

_____

_____

_____

_____

EXAMPLES:

I am rewarded for my initiative.
The company promotes creativity.
It is informal.
I am trusted with authority.
There are flexible hours.
I have a hands-off manager.
I have complete freedom and am totally accountable to myself.

3. What are the values of the organizations you've worked in that you liked?

If you've never liked an organization's values, describe what you *would* like.

Write here the values of the organizations you've worked in that you liked or you would like:

_____

_____

_____

_____

_____

_____

_____

_____

EXAMPLES:

They are supportive of employees.
They have the desire to do things better—to always improve.
Customers always come first.
People matter most.
Management communicates goals and expectations clearly.
They encourage personal growth among employees.
A patient's well-being is most important.
The focus is on helping people.

PONDER THIS

If you don't do what you dream of, how will you feel?

What do you risk if you don't do this?

How would your life be different if you did this?

SURVEY SHOWS PEOPLE WANT A BLEND OF WORK, LEISURE AND EDUCATION

People aren't just expecting to work longer, they want to mix work and leisure and learning and rest. That is one conclusion of the 2005 study The Future of Retirement, conducted by Harris Interactive with HSBC and Age Wave.

In 6 of the 10 societies surveyed, the majority said they saw the ideal "later lifestyle" as one in which they alternate between work and leisure. Specifically, here is how various societies view their later years:

▶ Canada: a time of reinvention, ambition and close relationships with friends and family

▶ America: a time for opportunity, new careers and spiritual fulfillment; less focus on family or health than other societies

▶ France: a time of dreams and aspirations, but also as a time of worry; they are concerned about being a burden to family

▶ Britain: a time of self-sufficiency, independence and personal responsibility

▶ Brazil: a time for slowing down, relaxing and spending time with family and friends; they expect support from their children

▶ Mexico: a time for continued work and hard-earned financial stability

▶ China: for younger generations, an opportunity for a new life but continued careers; for older generations, a time to stop working and relax

▶ Hong Kong: a time for rest, relaxation and the enjoyment of accumulated wealth, seen as the cornerstone of well-being

▶ India: a time to live with and be cared for by their families

▶ Japan: a time to look forward to where there is good health, family considerations and continued fulfillment from work

4. How do others describe you?

If you are having difficulty coming up with answers to some of these questions, feedback from other people who know you can help.

When my client Beth did this exercise, she said she "talked to other people to understand their perceptions about my strengths and interests. I ask them to reflect on and write down how they'd describe me. Having well-thought-out comments in a written form was very helpful. I paid special attention to similar statements made by different people."

So simply ask people who know you, "How would you describe me?" Another place to get this information is from past performance reviews. You can pick up themes and patterns that give insight into where you thrive, what you love to do and what is most important to you.

Write here how others describe you:

_____

_____

_____

_____

_____

_____

_____

_____

_____

_____

_____

_____

_____

_____

_____

_____

Examples of what people discovered about themselves by talking to others who know them:

> You are patient and caring.
> You do well with younger workers.
> You need autonomy.
> You are a born leader.
> You're good at business operations.
> You have a pioneer spirit.
> You are persuasive.
> You have a profound influence on others—
> especially one-on-one.
> Your sincere concern causes people to naturally want to share.

JERRY SPRINGER'S MANY CAREERS

▸ Began as a political aide to Robert F. Kennedy during his presidential campaign.

▸ Has been a lawyer and a five-term member of the Cincinnati City Council.

▸ Elected mayor of Cincinnati in 1977. At that time, he gave a daily morning radio address called *The Springer Memorandum.*

▸ Became a reporter and Emmy-winning news anchor and commentator and managing editor for WLWT-TV in Cincinnati.

▸ Sought the Democratic nomination for governor of Ohio.

▸ Started *The Jerry Springer Show* in 1991.

▸ At age 60, in 2005, began doing a radio show on Clear Channel radio, returning to his passion for public issues. "I've lived my life never shutting doors," he said in an April 2005 *New York Times* article.

5. Is there something you've always dreamed of doing?

Look back at that gnawing in the pit of your gut from Step 1. Did you capture it there? Or did any of these questions remind you of something you hadn't been in touch with before?

Write here what you've always dreamed of doing:

_____

_____

_____

_____

_____

_____

_____

_____

_____

_____

_____

HOW ONE MAN DEFINES SUCCESS

One definition of success is having more time to spend on the things you value outside of your work. Take Joel, a New York actor who went back to school to become a chiropractor at age 46. He told me, "Eventually I will have my own practice and can do what I want to do. It may even give me time to still do theater and be able to afford taking theater jobs for no money because my practice will be where I earn my keep."

Develop Part 1 of your new Career Objective

You are now ready to create Part 1 of your new career objective. This is not a job title. It is the result of the first steps you've taken in this process that help you describe what you might do, who you might do it with, and in what kind of environment you'd do it. This will evolve using the information you gather from each of the next three chapters.

Using the information you captured in Step 3 (your most joyful skills) and in the preceding five questions, write out the first part of your new career objective.

In my potential new career:

I'd (write your six most joyful skills here that you discovered in Step 3):

_____

_____

_____

_____

_____

_____

With (write the type of person, group or entity you might like to use your most joyful skills with that you just discovered in Step 4):

_____

_____

_____

_____

_____

_____

_____

Where I'd be (describe the environment and culture where you thrive that you just figured out in Step 4):

_____

_____

_____

_____

SAMPLE NEW CAREER OBJECTIVE, PART I

In my potential new career:

▶ I'd assess, advise, motivate, communicate with, create visuals for and counsel (your six most joyful skills) . . .

▶ self-motivated people who are unhappy with the way they look and feel (the type of person you might use your most joyful skills with) . . .

▶ where I'd be trusted to do a good job, challenged to always get better, rewarded for doing a good job and receive respectful feedback (the environment and culture where you'd thrive).

Write Part 1 of your new Career Objective here:

_____

_____

_____

_____

_____

_____

_____

_____

You may know Ben Stein from his deadpan delivery in such acting roles as the boring teacher in the movie *Ferris Bueller's Day Off*, or more recently as the host of the Comedy Central quiz show *Win Ben Stein's Money*. But acting is just one of his many careers.

He graduated with honors in economics from Columbia University and has been a lawyer, university adjunct professor and speechwriter for Richard Nixon and Gerald Ford. He's been a screenwriter, columnist and public speaker and has published 16 books—7 novels and 9 nonfiction books on finance and political and social issues of mass culture.

Why has he done so many things? Perhaps it has to do with what he wrote in his final column for E! Online: "Years ago, I realized I could never be as great an actor as Olivier or as good a comic as Steve Martin—or Martin Mull or Fred Willard—or as good an economist as Samuelson or Friedman or as good a writer as Fitzgerald."

He added, "I came to realize that life lived to help others is the only one that matters . . . This is my highest and best use as a human."

One more thing

In this step, you defined *who* you'd like to work with and the *environment* and *culture* you want to be in. The environment and culture will affect how you and others are treated. But you also want to clarify what's important to you in terms of your overall life so that your next career gives you the flexibility that fits your life and personal values. It is part of how you define success for yourself.

Early on, I discussed the purpose of changing careers: to have work that uses your strengths, challenges you, is meaningful, fits your values and personality and fits the life and future you want to create.

Well, this is the place where you define what "fits your life and future you want to create." For example, if at this point in life you want to work 30 hours a week, you want to figure that into your ideal situation. You may only want to work mornings so you can be available for your children in the afternoon or take a painting class. Or you may say that sitting down to eat dinner with your family every day is a priority. Or you want the flexibility to do more personal traveling.

Later on, when you're investigating and evaluating what you want to do, these will become the criteria to help you decide if a particular job makes sense based on what's most important to your overall life. You will clarify the "package" your new job comes in by defining your criteria.

So, write down any other criteria that are important to you:

_____

_____

_____

_____

_____

_____

_____

_____

_____

_____

_____

_____

_____

_____

_____

_____

▶ Almost 4 out of 10 women who left the workforce and then returned said they chose careers with fewer responsibilities and lower pay to have time for their families, according to a 2005 survey by the Center for Work-Life Policy. Of the women surveyed, 40 percent took full-time professional positions, and about 10 percent went to work for themselves.

▶ In another survey, conducted in 2005 by Salary.com, 39 percent of respondents said that if given the choice, they would choose more time off instead of a $5,000 raise. This is a nearly 20 percent increase from what respondents said in 2001.

▶ In looking at what's most important to the younger generation—those in their early to mid-20s—quality time with family and friends is a priority and making an impact on the world is more important than how much money they'll make, according to Northwestern Mutual's Millennium Generation Study conducted in 2004.

Step 5

Name what you know about.

At the end of my third meeting with Beth, the engineer, I told her to go home and write out everything she knows about. She looked at me like I was crazy. She did it anyway, and it was an eye-opening exercise that quickly took her to the next phase of her career-change process.

Now, I want you to do the same thing: Write out everything you know about. What I mean by this is: Think about the knowledge you have accumulated over the years. For example, if you've been a manager, you probably know about human-resource issues, including hiring and performance reviews, training, presentations, team development and budgets, to name a few.

If you've been a public-relations person at nonprofit organizations, you might know about things such as grant writing, donor recognition programs, special events, public speaking, corporate partnerships, volunteer management and direct-mail solicitation. If you've been in sales, you might know about pricing, contracts, marketing, territory management, proposals, customer service, new product launches and vendor relations.

Or, if you've been a manager in public radio, you might know about fundraising and development, media relations, board and community relations, staffing and hiring, budgets, purchasing, engineering, classical music, project management, grants and endowments, digital radio transition, recording facilities and programming.

But don't limit this exercise to work. Think about what you know from other areas of your life. What other activities have you been involved in, and what knowledge did you gain from those? Do you know about mentoring, art, Latin culture, reflexology, nutrition, leadership, gardening, animal training, presentations, parenting, politics, history, education or dance?

You should be able to come up with several columns of knowledge—even pages.

So, to discover what you know, here are the questions to answer:

1. Quite simply, what do you know about? What knowledge have you accumulated?

Even if you don't think something is relevant, a big deal or useful to know, write it down.

Write here what you know about:

_____

_____

_____

_____

_____

_____

_____

_____

_____

_____

_____

_____

_____

_____

_____

_____

_____

_____

If you get stuck, here are examples of things you might know about:

financial services
new product development
emerging technology
commodities trading
contract negotiation
antiques
business turnarounds
vendor relations
competitive showing of horses
manufacturing
quality systems
EPA and OSHA regulations
business plans
fundraising
film
biofeedback
stress management
meditation
licensing
model making
popular culture
fabric
point-of-purchase displays
logos
annual reports
imports and exports
sales, marketing and strategic
    planning
training
human resources
budgets
teams
writing manuals and
    operational procedures
global work environments
presentations

educational outreach and
    programming
sociological theory
media
copy writing
meeting and event planning
gourmet cooking
logistics
behavioral patterns
working with volunteers
investment portfolio management
tax planning
retirement and employee bene-
    fit planning
estate planning
charitable gifting strategies
federal tax code and legislation
equipment procurement
support desks
alternative medicine
database and software design
security related to electronic
    data and hardware networks
building modification guidelines
neuroscience
biophysics
drug discovery process
modeling
project management
accounting
management
vitamins and supplements
small business development
operations
advertising
consulting

2. What do you want to know more about? What are you curious about?

Poking around in your head and asking yourself what you'd like to know *more* about can give you new data and expand your thinking.

When I made a career change, I knew a lot about communication, self-improvement, language, presentations, writing, positioning and promotion. But I was extremely curious about human behavior, goal setting, careers, inspiration and hope.

Knowing this helped me piece together part of the puzzle of my new career. By looking at what I was most curious about, I started to see what I might communicate and write about and how my knowl-

When asked what other careers sounded most appealing to them, attorneys had this to say, according to a 2005 survey conducted by Robert Half Legal:

▶ Mediation or alternative dispute-resolution counselor: **54 percent**

▶ Law school professor or lecturer: **49 percent**

▶ Nonprofit or public-interest legal services provider: **41 percent**

▶ Expert witness: **20 percent**

▶ Patent expert: **11 percent**

▶ Researcher: **11 percent**

▶ Politician, such as district attorney or attorney general: **9 percent**

edge could be applied in a new way with subject material that really fascinated me.

Another way to look at this question is to ask yourself what you think you need to learn more about to develop into the kind of person you want to be. Think about my client Jerry. The issues that were so prominent in his life and ones he had worked on were how to lose weight, stop smoking and develop a healthier, happier lifestyle.

He was incessantly curious about how to do that, had done some self-study and created a healthier and happier life for himself. He lost more than 100 pounds, changed his diet, began an exercise program and developed new, healthy habits. When we talked about what he wanted to know more about, he discovered that he wanted a deeper understanding of relaxation techniques, anatomy, physiology, disease, stress, dietetics, root causes of overeating, why people don't take care of themselves and how to motivate them.

Write here what you want to know more about or are curious about:

_____

_____

_____

_____

_____

_____

_____

_____

_____

_____

_____

_____

_____

Organize what you know about into four to six key categories

You should now have lists of words. So, let's organize them by creating up to six categories in which to put these words.

For example, Beth came back with three pages of knowledge that she categorized into four areas: Engineering, Business, Hobby and Software. Under Engineering, she placed things like aeromechanics, statistics, analytical modeling, test coverage and monitoring. Under outside interests and hobbies, she placed such topics as: wireless communication technology, digital technologies, audio/video components and color theory.

After Beth categorized her knowledge into four areas, she said, "This helped me realize that I know more than I think I do and that was very motivating."

My client Jerry came up with a master list of words that he categorized into six subject areas: food/nutrition, health, exercise/sports, computers, small business and marketing. Then he listed specifics that fit into those categories that he pulled from his master list. Under Food and Nutrition, he placed such topics as cooking methods, safety, seasoning, diets, benefits of vegetarianism, how nutrients work and proper protein consumption. Under Exercise, he placed cardiovascular and weight training and optimal aerobic training and running.

Develop Part 2 of your new Career Objective

Using the new information you captured here—your knowledge organized into categories (and yet-to-be-learned knowledge on subjects you are curious about)—write out Part 2 of your new career objective. Transfer what you wrote at the end of Step 4 in Part 1 of your new Career Objective and add the new information you have discovered here.

In my potential new career,

I'd (write your six most joyful skills):

_____

_____

_____

_____

_____

_____

With (write the type of person, group or entity you might like to use your most joyful skills with):

_____

_____

_____

Where I'd be (describe the environment and culture where you thrive):

_____

_____

_____

_____

Incorporating my knowledge about and interest in (write what you know about):

_____

_____

_____

_____

Sample new Career Objective, with Part 2

In my potential new career:

▶ I'd assess, advise, motivate, communicate with, create visuals for and counsel (your six most joyful skills) . . .

▶ self-motivated people who are unhappy with the way they look and feel (the type of person you might use your most joyful skills with) . . .

▶ where I'd be trusted to do a good job, challenged to always get better, rewarded for doing a good job and receive respectful feedback (the environment and culture where you'd thrive) . . .

▶ incorporating my knowledge about (and interest in) diet, nutrition, exercise, stress management, working with the public, small-business development and operations and marketing (what you know about).

Write your new Career Objective with Part 2 here:

Step 6

Say what you
care about.

ow often does someone ask you what you care about? It matters *a lot* when it comes to your new, satisfying career. So, this is the place to think about the issues, trends and problems you care about in life. These may overlap with the knowledge you listed or things you're curious about that you defined in Step 5. That's fine. It tells us you're in the right zone.

Answering these questions can give you a lot of insight into your-self—not to mention that you'll probably get excited just thinking about things that matter to you. When it comes to work, most people don't even consider this. They think of work as work. The place you go to do a job. Yet doing work that evolves around something you *care* about can be one of the most crucial parts of having a meaningful and satisfying career.

A man who had been an advertising copywriter most of his career told me how he liked writing and giving words impact, but didn't care about advertising. As a result, he wasn't very satisfied or energized about his work.

When I asked him what he did care about, he paused for a second and then said, "Stories." We talked about whether he could see himself using his ability to write and persuade through the creation of stories. It was as if I were talking to a different person.

A world of possibilities had opened up to him, and he could see himself fitting in. Thinking about what he cared about most helped him begin to tie together everything he had discovered about himself up to this point.

You start this step by answering these questions: What matters to you most? What issues, trends, institutions, causes and problems do you care about?

Go back to my client Jerry, the bookstore employee, who knew he wanted to help people. When I asked him to name the issues, trends, institutions, causes and problems he cared most about he mentioned fitness, nutrition, healthy lifestyles, obesity and diabetes. Many of the issues he cared most about were ones he had personally struggled with, including fitness, nutrition and creating a healthy lifestyle.

"First I wrote down several pages of 'stuff,' like chairs of all sorts, home automation, containers, PDAs, customized things, watches with unconventional functionality, automated bill payments, coffee grinder that grinds and brews, automatic litter box. Then I wrote down categories that I felt summarized the pages and came up with words like technology; aesthetics; things that are useful, functional, logical; daily home life; features. This was one of the most significant realizations I made in my journey. I realized that I could actually be passionate about something."

Seeing this on paper helped him realize how deeply he cared about these things. He also began to see a common thread throughout what he *cared about*, what he *knew about* and was *curious about* and how he might apply his *most joyful skills*. In our fifth meeting, as we reviewed the list of issues, trends and problems he cared about, I could feel the momentum churning in him and lights starting to go off inside his head about the possibilities of what he might do next.

As with the last step, where you wrote down what you know about, thinking of all the things that you might care about can feel overwhelming. To help you tackle it, I've organized the various segments of life into 26 categories. Trust me, I have not thought of everything; but it's a start. Feel free to create your own categories.

Within these 26 categories, I've created subcategories. Some subcategories can fit into other broader categories. Use these as a guide. As you read through this list, check off the categories and subcategories you care most about.

Various Categories of Life

(Check off what you care most about)

HEALTH
- ☐ aging
- ☐ stress
- ☐ nutrition
- ☐ fitness
- ☐ exercise
- ☐ diet
- ☐ disease
- ☐ weight training
- ☐ lifestyle
- ☐ other: _____
- ☐ other: _____

HEALTH CARE
- ☐ cost
- ☐ access to
- ☐ delivery of
- ☐ drugs
- ☐ alternative medicine
- ☐ treatment
- ☐ other: _____
- ☐ other: _____

ENVIRONMENT
- ☐ climate
- ☐ nuclear waste
- ☐ environmental hazards
- ☐ ecosystems
- ☐ waste disposal
- ☐ toxic waste ecosystems
- ☐ species
- ☐ farming techniques
- ☐ habitats

- ☐ pollution
- ☐ resources
- ☐ water and food supply
- ☐ oil spills
- ☐ recycling
- ☐ gardening
- ☐ ecology
- ☐ horticulture technology
- ☐ landscaping
- ☐ other: _____
- ☐ other: _____

PUBLIC HEALTH
- ☐ infant mortality
- ☐ AIDS
- ☐ world hunger
- ☐ disease
- ☐ genocide
- ☐ viruses
- ☐ population growth and longevity
- ☐ other: _____
- ☐ other: _____

GLOBAL CIVILIZATION
- ☐ societal economics
- ☐ economic globalization
- ☐ human rights
- ☐ poverty
- ☐ social change
- ☐ world peace
- ☐ justice
- ☐ other: _____
- ☐ other: _____

FAMILY

- ☐ balance
- ☐ marriage
- ☐ reproduction and family planning
- ☐ child care
- ☐ elder care
- ☐ parenting
- ☐ adoption
- ☐ end-of-life care
- ☐ other: _____
- ☐ other: _____

BUSINESS

- ☐ management
- ☐ leadership
- ☐ crisis management
- ☐ conflict resolution
- ☐ human resources
- ☐ productivity
- ☐ creativity
- ☐ finance
- ☐ corporate governance
- ☐ advertising
- ☐ real estate
- ☐ intellectual property
- ☐ nonprofit
- ☐ sales and marketing
- ☐ project management
- ☐ world markets
- ☐ product competition
- ☐ branding
- ☐ venture capital
- ☐ entrepreneurship
- ☐ knowledge management
- ☐ other: _____
- ☐ other: _____

WORK

- ☐ career choice
- ☐ multigenerational work force
- ☐ unions
- ☐ work/life balance
- ☐ ergonomics
- ☐ retirement
- ☐ personal finance
- ☐ transitions
- ☐ mentoring
- ☐ diversity
- ☐ other: _____
- ☐ other: _____

ENERGY

- ☐ solar
- ☐ utilities
- ☐ petroleum, gasoline, electric
- ☐ nuclear
- ☐ renewable resources
- ☐ water supplies
- ☐ fossil fuels
- ☐ fuel cell–powered cars
- ☐ other: _____
- ☐ other: _____

SECURITY

- ☐ terrorism
- ☐ privacy
- ☐ computers
- ☐ homeland security
- ☐ travel and transportation
- ☐ infrastructure
- ☐ food safety
- ☐ emergency management
- ☐ other: _____
- ☐ other: _____

ANIMALS
- [ ] extinction
- [ ] care of
- [ ] behavior
- [ ] communications
- [ ] rights
- [ ] training
- [ ] health
- [ ] welfare
- [ ] other: _____
- [ ] other: _____

FOOD
- [ ] vegetarianism
- [ ] gourmet
- [ ] preparation
- [ ] serving
- [ ] catering
- [ ] wine
- [ ] safety
- [ ] entertainment
- [ ] special events
- [ ] other: _____
- [ ] other: _____

SPIRITUALITY
- [ ] faith
- [ ] interfaith relations
- [ ] customs
- [ ] theology
- [ ] religion
- [ ] scriptures
- [ ] other: _____
- [ ] other: _____

ECONOMICS
- [ ] trends
- [ ] forecasts
- [ ] inflation
- [ ] interest rates
- [ ] employment levels
- [ ] mathematical models
- [ ] business cycles
- [ ] tax legislation
- [ ] statistics
- [ ] currency
- [ ] market research
- [ ] imports and exports
- [ ] eco-economy
- [ ] other: _____
- [ ] other: _____

GOVERNMENT
- [ ] world affairs
- [ ] politics
- [ ] laws and public policy
- [ ] world governance
- [ ] monetary policy
- [ ] democracy
- [ ] altruism
- [ ] other: _____
- [ ] other: _____

SOCIETY
- [ ] lifestyles
- [ ] values
- [ ] equality
- [ ] women
- [ ] diversity
- [ ] cultural differences
- [ ] behavior
- [ ] ethics
- [ ] personal freedom
- [ ] human rights
- [ ] children
- [ ] marriage

- [ ] quality of life
- [ ] convenience
- [ ] downshifting
- [ ] consumerism
- [ ] other: _____
- [ ] other: _____

LEISURE & ENTERTAINMENT

- [ ] travel
- [ ] sports
- [ ] hobbies
- [ ] music
- [ ] dance
- [ ] film
- [ ] art
- [ ] acting
- [ ] theater
- [ ] video games
- [ ] other: _____
- [ ] other: _____

STYLE

- [ ] fashion
- [ ] beauty
- [ ] hair
- [ ] makeup
- [ ] couture
- [ ] other: _____
- [ ] other: _____

CULTURE

- [ ] art
- [ ] music
- [ ] aesthetics
- [ ] design
- [ ] literature
- [ ] other: _____
- [ ] other: _____

COMMUNICATIONS

- [ ] media
- [ ] free speech
- [ ] graphics
- [ ] advertising
- [ ] public relations
- [ ] language
- [ ] interpreting and translation
- [ ] publishing
- [ ] news
- [ ] new media
- [ ] other: _____
- [ ] other: _____

EDUCATION

- [ ] public
- [ ] higher education
- [ ] literacy
- [ ] teacher education
- [ ] curricula
- [ ] testing
- [ ] other: _____
- [ ] other: _____

TECHNOLOGY

- [ ] innovation
- [ ] mobile marketplace and technology
- [ ] cybernetics
- [ ] robotics
- [ ] cloning
- [ ] artificial intelligence
- [ ] Internet
- [ ] gadgets
- [ ] biotechnology
- [ ] genomics
- [ ] home automation products
- [ ] other: _____
- [ ] other: _____

SCIENCE

- ☐ biological enhancements
- ☐ genetics and genetic engineering
- ☐ space flight including commercializing, private efforts and space enterprise
- ☐ biology
- ☐ chemistry
- ☐ physics
- ☐ bioengineered food
- ☐ other: _____
- ☐ other: _____

COMMUNITY

- ☐ social movements
- ☐ city planning
- ☐ transportation
- ☐ regional economic development
- ☐ infrastructure
- ☐ tourism
- ☐ neighborhoods
- ☐ other: _____
- ☐ other: _____

PSYCHOLOGY

- ☐ emotional intelligence
- ☐ behavior
- ☐ relationships
- ☐ compassion
- ☐ respect
- ☐ responsibility
- ☐ personal growth
- ☐ other: _____
- ☐ other: _____
- ☐ other: _____

WOMEN'S ISSUES

- ☐ balance
- ☐ relationships
- ☐ careers
- ☐ equality
- ☐ fertility
- ☐ osteoporosis
- ☐ breast cancer
- ☐ menopause
- ☐ other: _____
- ☐ other: _____
- ☐ other: _____

Nicholas D. Snider, a former senior vice president at UPS, created his next career based on something he had cared about his entire life. A lifelong collector of patriotic artifacts, such as jewelry, flags and banners, Nicholas announced his idea to start a nonprofit organization in 1997 dedicated to promoting the history of patriotism. Through his efforts, he founded the Museum of Patriotism.

Write the areas that you care most about here:

_____

_____

_____

_____

_____

_____

_____

_____

_____

_____

_____

_____

_____

_____

_____

_____

_____

_____

_____

_____

_____

_____

_____

_____

_____

_____

_____

How a construction guy became an ad executive

Will was a contractor who specialized in redoing houses. Two specific events had such an impact on Will that they became the impetus for his career change. One was the recession that essentially annihilated the construction business he was in, with interest rates and inflation above 20 percent in 1981. The other event was when the police raided his wedding, which was held in a public park.

"My two young nephews had climbed on the roof of a lodge and the caretaker called the police. It escalated out of control. The police closed down the wedding reception and threatened my sixth-grade teacher and sister-in-law with jail and arrested two relatives. I've always believed in our Constitution. I concluded, on the grand scale, our government was out of control and was ruining life economically.

"Locally, the police were out of control. My government didn't reflect the values and Constitution of America. I was faced with a decision to ignore it or try to do something about it. So, I decided to get involved in politics.

"I began going to city council meetings and public hearings on issues that impacted people. When it was time for citizen input, I'd get up and speak my mind. I was always quoted the next day in the paper. I'd research an issue and introduce alternative approaches to problems like panhandling and electric rate increases. After one forum, a city council member asked me for my research on alternative public transportation and introduced my idea at council. I discovered my ideas had weight and the ability to change the public dialogue, and I could assimilate complex stuff and communicate it in two minutes or less in a powerful way. I set out to make a difference in government and I was doing it.

"A local political party approached me to run as a city council candidate. I led the opposition to the biggest issue of the election, which put me in the news at least once a week for six months. Every letter to the editor I wrote was published.

"Even though I didn't get elected, I discovered I had persuasive writing skills and great instincts. But I needed to rethink what I was doing. I discovered it wasn't possible to be elected just on the strength of your ideas. It took campaign finances I'd never have. But I knew something had been unleashed in me. I had been a creative writing major in

Kathy Stevens was a teacher and curriculum trainer moving up in her field. She was named principal of a new charter school in Boston, but the job just didn't feel right and she left it. She loved animals and teaching, and decided to join the two things she cared so much about into a new career. In 2001, she created the Catskill Animal Sanctuary, which provides shelter for abused, abandoned and neglected horses and farm animals, finds them homes and educates children and others about treatment of the animals through on-site and school programming.

college and went back to evening college and took marketing communications. Every advertising project I did for class was named the best. I realized there was a fit in corporate America for what I did well.

"Then another local political issue came up and I was asked by a city council member who I'd run against to head the opposition group to that issue and develop the strategy and ads. That was my first paid consulting role in public relations and advertising, and we won by 73 percent of the vote. I was asked to head up another issue, which was successful, and in that process, I met a man who owned an advertising agency. When I saw an ad in the paper for a media buyer for this guy's company, I called him. He said the position was clerical but that he was looking for someone he could groom to handle client management.

"This job would be a big leap because I was still seen as a construction guy. We had five interviews—all at restaurants. I still had a 1974 pickup truck and would park two blocks away so he couldn't see it. He could see that I had done issue management and had public-relations skills, and finally he hired me as an account executive. The first day, I brought in my own typewriter. I did well and developed my skills as an advertising copywriter and worked on more political campaigns. Within two years, I was vice president.

"You know the saying, 'It's not what you know, it's who you know?' It's a cop-out attitude. It's about who you are, what you do and how strongly and passionately you pursue where you want to go."

How a software engineer became a chef

Leonard was a software analyst who liked to make money. And he had done that for the first few years of his career working for a consumer-products company and an insurance firm.

He was 21 years old and weighed 310 pounds. On November 2, 1998, he woke up with swollen ankles. "I had to do something about it," he declared.

"I decided I would lose 130 pounds, and achieved that in about 13 months," he said. "Until then I had no interest in food and didn't care about the quality, only consuming it. I became a certified personal trainer, did nutrition research and took nutrition classes while I finished my degree in information systems and business administration and worked in my job as a software analyst."

Leonard wasn't particularly unhappy in his work. "But the more I learned about nutrition, the more I became intrigued, and once I started cooking, there was a snowball effect. I wanted to understand anything and everything about food to make the best, healthiest food I could. I was a Food Network addict. I spent all my free time in grocery stores—four to five hours—memorizing labels to understand the nutritional aspects and what the end product would be like when I combined various foods.

"Something sparked my right brain, although I didn't think I had any artistic talent. One day I started to make really good stuff and my artistic side presented itself. I made deviled quail eggs with white truffles and prosciutto to take to someone's house.

"Everyone was oohing and aahing. They were blown away, overwhelmed with the variety and depth of flavor."

He began to think about what it would be like to make food for a living and had many discussions with his wife, to whom he had only been married a short time. "We talked about what we'd have to give up financially and time-wise if I was to change careers."

One afternoon they were at a local shopping mall, when his wife saw a sign in the women's restroom for a whole-food grocery store. It read, LOOKING FOR PASSIONATE HOME COOKS TO TEACH COOKING CLASSES.

Leonard applied, and ended up teaching students how to make citrus-glazed chicken. He loved the experience, but was still working as a software analyst. Before he made the decision to change careers, he wanted to know what he'd be getting into. So, while working full-time during the day, he worked at a restaurant two nights a week for free.

"I told them I'll do anything, I just wanted to understand the business. Everything I'd seen on TV glamorized it and I wanted to see the difference between sitting in a cubicle and working in a kitchen. I had no restaurant experience other than scooping out milkshakes at a Steak and Shake when I was fifteen."

For about a month, he worked in this restaurant's kitchen doing everything from cutting vegetables for the chef and assembling dishes to learning how to build flavor in sauces.

"Mostly, I asked questions nonstop. I was there to learn anything and everything. It further cemented my love of food. This was a humungous decision for me and I wanted to make sure it was the right one. No pun intended, but it whet my palate."

He decided to enroll in culinary school and attended one semester but was bored.

"I saw a job posting at a restaurant for A.M. Pantry Position. I asked my professor, 'Do you think I can get it?' and he said, 'I doubt it, since you have no experience.' But I contacted the chef anyway.

"He agreed to talk to me the next day for fifteen minutes. I was overdressed and had a completely irrelevant resume. I told him, 'I have no restaurant experience and no culinary skills, but I have more passion, a better work ethic and more desire than anyone you'll bring into this room.' He said, 'Oh.' Then we spoke for four hours. He wanted

> "I'm not only using my strengths, but every day, I'm involved in what I care about: relationships, becoming a better person, compassion, respect, personal responsibility and growth and psychology. It feels like who I am and what I should be doing."
>
> **BETH ANN,**
> who became a psychotherapist after 17 years as an interior designer

to see if I was as into it as I said. I was hired on the spot. That day I gave my two-week notice at work.

"My parents were freaked out. I had to give up time with my wife, who I'd been married to less than a year. The chef let me work the salad station from seven A.M. to two P.M. He baby-stepped me into everything. I made a meager hourly wage now. But I learned more in the first week in the restaurant than I had learned in four months of school. The chef was phenomenal—the time investment he put into me. He was hard on me, but believed in me and shared so much information. Today he is like a brother to me."

When the chef left that restaurant, Leonard followed.

To learn how other kitchens operated, he worked in three Chicago restaurants, free, as a *stagiare*, someone who "observes the kitchen as a student of the art" and who does whatever needs to be done.

Today he works as a co-sous chef in a restaurant he describes as a "tapa-style, eclectic mix of multicultural tastes" that's based in Mason, Ohio, and is listed as one of America's top restaurants in the 2005 Zagat survey.

Besides working up to 70 hours a week at the restaurant, he also teaches three to four classes a month.

"I get so much pleasure out of food and I want to share it with others," he said. "It's intense, but I get to go in and play with food every day. I love it."

HOW AN EXECUTIVE ASSISTANT IS BECOMING A PERFORMER

I first heard from Pamela Mitchell in the fall of 2005 after she had read one of my articles. She wrote to say, "I am at the point in my life when I can no longer work without passion. I am 44 years old, have a 14-year-old daughter, am divorced and working as an executive assistant in a very corporate environment.

"Recently I decided to 'redeem' my lifelong dream of being a film actress." This five-foot, seven-inch, blue-eyed woman whom others describe as "a brunette Marilyn Monroe" said she used her "know-how from watching my older sister, who was a professional model, to get head shots done, create a resume and mail them to several talent agencies in Atlanta. So far, I've gotten callbacks from two, both wanting to represent me.

"I also expressed my interest in pursuing my passion to a close friend who introduced me to the writer/director of several films and I decided to join Women in Film/Atlanta to network with other women in the industry."

Over the past 15 years, Pamela has dabbled in acting in commercials, as a movie extra and in a role in an independent film as an FBI agent. When she was in her 20s, she was a singer in a rock band and later sang jazz, and rhythm and blues.

Eight months after I first heard from her, after she read an article on branding, she changed her name to something that would be "more unique and recognizable," she said. She is now Merritt Mitchell, named after her grandfather.

"I signed with Atlanta Models and Talent, and they have been sending me on 'go-sees' for print work and commercials. I just entered the *More Magazine*/Wilhelmina Models 40+ Model Search." Besides getting exposure, she hopes to win a modeling contract.

She's most excited about the fact that she created a jingle for her company, a fast-food restaurant franchise that was recently acquired by the parent company.

THE PATH WITH A HEART

"Does this path have a heart? If it does, the path is good; if it doesn't, it is of no use. Both paths lead nowhere; but one has a heart; the other doesn't. One makes for a joyful journey; as long as you follow it, you are one with it. The other will make you curse your life. One makes you strong; the other weakens you. A path without heart is never enjoyable. You have to work hard even to take it. On the other hand, a path with heart is easy; it does not make you work at liking it."

CARLOS CASTANEDA, from *A Yaqui Warrior*

"I went to the senior vice president of marketing, shut the door to his office and sang it to him. He loved it."

In the meantime, she's waiting to get her bonus for the work she does at her day job so she can develop a "comp card"—a compilation of her different photographs—which costs about $1,000, to further market herself.

"I'm just playing and seeing where it all goes," she said. "Every day it seems to become more and more a reality. I am looking forward to work that I can't get enough of and would never dream of retiring from. None of us wants to look back and say shoulda, coulda, woulda."

No title, please

You may have noticed that although we've been developing a career objective as we go through these steps, we have never talked about a *job title*. Yes, eventually, you will call yourself something. At some point, you may need to put a label to what you're seeking. But for now, no titles.

You're creating a *picture* of what you want based on your skills and interests and the environment in which you want to apply those. Remember, to do this right, you need to see yourself as a body of skills, not a title. Even if you're champing at the bit to give yourself a title, please refrain. It only limits you.

Of course, I understand why you may want to do that. Label making is something people do to help themselves and others easily understand where they fit into the world. And it starts young. A 17-year-old who worked at the M.I.T. Media Lab wrote this about his future plans in an essay in *The New York Times Magazine*: "I don't know what I want to do exactly, but I wouldn't feel bad labeling myself as an inventor."

There are a dozen different ways he might fit into the workplace. Labels limit. Keep it open for now.

Instead of a title that boxes you in, you have created so much more up to now: an understanding and sense of what matters to you most and what you might actually do every day to be involved with that. For now and the immediate future, you don't need to be crystal clear. Just clear enough that you could recognize the essence of it if you saw it.

No matter how old you are or what your circumstances, you're never out of options to do what you dream to do. My 42-year-old client who was in sales had wanted to be a doctor when he was in his 20s. Twenty years later, he decided to follow that dream—but with a twist. Since he didn't want to go to medical school, he set out to explore how he could make a difference in the world of medicine. He knew his strongest skills were his ability to communicate effectively, persuade, organize data and inspire others to take action. He wanted to use those skills with something he cared about. He is taking steps to become a medical educator with a focus on Crohn's disease—something he has had personal experience with in his own life and cares about deeply.

Develop Part 3 of your new Career Objective

Incorporating the new information you captured here—the issues you care most about—write Part 3 of your new career objective.
In my potential new career:

I'd (write your six most joyful skills):

_____

_____

_____

_____

_____

_____

With (write the type of person, group or entity you might like to use your most joyful skills with):

_____

_____

_____

_____

Where I'd be (describe the environment and culture where you thrive):

_____

_____

_____

_____

Incorporating my knowledge about and interest in (write what you know about):

_____

_____

_____

_____

By applying my passion for or interest in (write what you care about):

_____

_____

_____

_____

_____

Sample new Career Objective, with Part 3

In my potential new career:

- I'd assess, advise, motivate, communicate with, create visuals for and counsel (your six most joyful skills) . . .

- self-motivated people who are unhappy with the way they look and feel (the type of person you might use your most joyful skills with) . . .

- where I'd be trusted to do a good job, challenged to always get better, rewarded for doing a good job and receive respectful feedback (the environment and culture where you'd thrive) . . .

- incorporating my knowledge about diet, nutrition, exercise, stress management, working with the public, small business development and operations and marketing (what you know about) . . .

- by applying my passion for or interest in healthy lifestyles, wellness and education (what you care about).

(Someone who has this objective might be a counselor, dietician, public speaker, fitness coach, medical professional or many other things. But you guessed it, we're not ready to give it a name. We still need more information, which we'll get into next.)

Write your new Career Objective with Part 3 here:

_____

_____

_____

_____

_____

_____

_____

_____

_____

Step 7

Find what's new,
what's happening and
where you'd fit.

U p to now, you've spent most of your energy focusing on yourself. It's time to explore the rest of the world and spot trends and issues and the possibilities of where you fit into that world.

Before we do that, let's review what you've learned and have incorporated into your new, evolving career objective. We know:

- What gnaws at you
- What you like doing most
- The environment and culture you'd thrive in
- Who you might like to work around or with
- What you know
- What you care about

Let's see how your developing objective matches up with what's happening in the areas you said you care about most in Step 6.

You're going to do this through three activities:

1. Brain-tapping (yours)
2. Online and book research
3. Brain-tapping (others)

As you perform these three activities, you'll be discovering such things as:

- Possible ways to be involved in the areas you care about
- Issues and trends surrounding the areas you care about
- What's driving these areas in the direction they're going in
- How the above match up with your new career objective

> *"I say to myself that if it can be imagined,*
> *it can be created."*
>
> RODERICK ROMERO, creator of ecofriendly treehouses and former lead singer of the Seattle band Sky Cries Mary

Activity 1: Brain-tapping (yours)

A. On a blank sheet of paper, write what you *think* people involved in one area you care most about might do. For example, let's say one of the areas you said you cared most about was politics.

Off the top of your head, what do you think are some ways to be involved in politics? These might include:

- running for office
- political or editorial writing
- lobbying
- managing political campaigns
- creating political strategy
- working in government, including domestic or foreign affairs
- creating public policy for a think tank
- handling public relations

Another way to look at this is to ask: What's involved in politics? Who's involved? There's no one single question to ask to get started. But if you're stuck, ask someone to brainstorm with you.

B. Look at the list you just came up with. What entries appeal to you? You may not know exactly what a lobbyist does yet, but if it attracts you, circle it.

C. Think about what a lobbyist might do and write what you *guess* the work would be like. Include:

1. The skills this person would use
2. What the environment and culture where a lobbyist works would be like
3. Who a lobbyist works with
4. What a lobbyist needs to know about or have an interest in knowing more about

This gets you thinking about what this area might be like—even picturing yourself working in it. It also gives you a beginning point for your research and to see how close your assessment is to reality.

As another example, what if you said that one of the things you care about is animals. So what do you think are some ways to be involved with animals? These might include:

- care and treatment
- training
- protection
- animal rights
- education related to animals
- research related to animals
- foundations that support animals
- directing a facility that shelters animals
- pet sitting and transporting of animals
- animal communications
- lobbying for humane treatment of animals
- working with wildlife
- photographing, drawing or writing about animals

What on your list appeals to you? What would someone in this area do? What skills do you think they'd use? What would someone need to know about or have an interest in knowing more about?

NEW LAWS AND REGULATIONS MAKE FOR POTENTIAL JOBS

Depending on what the new laws are and who they affect, many people and businesses may need help to comply. For example, Federal Communications Commission rules require that most English-language broadcast, cable and satellite programming be closed captioned by January 2006. According to Brenda McSwigan of the distance-learning school National Professions, Inc., in Lantana, Florida, and Hearinglossweb.com, there are not enough "captioners" to fill the jobs to provide the services broadcasters will need.

What if you're interested in the elderly? What do you think are some ways to be involved? These might be:

- family caregiving
- mental health and autonomy
- medical care and care management
- living arrangements
- end-of-life care
- financial well-being
- pain management
- prevention
- delivery of needed services

What on your list appeals to you? Could someone specialize in a particular area? For instance, what would someone who assists with the financial well-being of the elderly do? Is there a way to combine your interest in the elderly with your interest in finances? What skills do you think a person in this area might use? What would someone need to know about or have an interest in knowing more about?

Now, let's plunge into a little research to see if your conception matches up with reality.

Activity 2: Online and book research

It may seem that the next logical step is to talk to people and find out more about your areas of interest. You certainly could do that at this point. But if you wait until after you've done this next activity, you'll have more intelligent, focused and fruitful conversations later. Here's why.

Right now, you've got a limited amount of information and knowledge. Even though it may seem easier to simply ask someone what you want to know, people are busy and don't have time to give you a complete education.

There's nothing more frustrating for someone than to get a call from you saying, "I want to get into the film industry. Can you tell me where to start?" They would want to help, and they might agree to talk to you; but there's too much ground to cover for the conversation to be as effective as you need it to be. You might even be frustrated because people don't know how to help you at this early stage, and they would be more inclined to help you if your request isn't overwhelming for them.

What if you could say, "I've been researching the film industry and I am exploring how to best utilize my skills as a manager of people and projects in several areas in this field. I have pinpointed a few directions, but need advice. Would you be willing to give me some input?" That's the point you'll be at if you complete this next activity first.

So, instead of calling people, go online or dig up articles, books and other published sources to help you discover:

- What's involved in the area you care about and appeals to you most
- What kinds of jobs might exist in this area
- What trends are affecting this area

This will begin to help prove or disprove what you think (based on your own brainstorming) and expand your knowledge. As a result, you will be better informed when you sit down and talk to someone. You can find information by reading consumer and trade publications, doing general searches online and going to market research or opinion sites, such as Gallup's and Web sites that write about cultural trends (see list of sources on trends, opposite page).

To illustrate how to do a general online search, I'll use our "politics" example. I begin my research by being very specific, typing into a search engine, "lobbyist," "lobbying" or "foreign affairs jobs."

Or you might be more general, typing in terms such as:

- jobs in politics
- political employment recruiters (this can help you learn about what jobs exist in politics)
- associations and special interest organizations
- political campaigns
- government jobs
- public policy organizations
- political party headquarters
- political magazines and journals

Sources for trends and other data

- Futurist.com
- Trendsetters.com
- The World Future Society
- *The Futurist* magazine
- Trendwatching.com, an Amsterdam-based trend agency
- U.S. Bureau of Labor Statistics (www.bls.gov)
- U.S. Census Bureau
- U.S. Statistical Abstract (www.census.gov/statab)
- Trade publications
- Consumer magazines
- *The Popcorn Report,* by Faith Popcorn
- American Demographics (analyzes trends and consumer insights as a monthly report in *Ad Age* and AdAge.com)
- *Fast Company* magazine
- *Fortune* magazine
- *Utne* (formerly *Utne Reader*)
- New laws and regulations
- What people discuss every day and consistently need or complain about
- Institute for the Future (research group focusing on consumers, technology, health and health care, workplace and global business trends)
- Strategic News Source (trends on computing and telecommunications)
- *Popular Science* magazine (developments in science, technology, automotive and electronics)
- Worldwatch Institute (research "for an environmentally sustainable and socially just society")
- Sciencedaily.com
- *Futuring: The Exploration of the Future,* a book by Edward Cornish

While you may not find out all of the following, here's the type of information to look for (take notes and print out data you think you'll refer to later):

- What people do in this area or areas
- The kinds of jobs that exist
- Skills people use in the roles or jobs that sound appealing
- What the environment and culture of the work and such organization are like
- Who interacts with people in this work
- The kind of knowledge that is important to have or acquire
- Ideals, education or experience people in these areas or particular jobs have
- Trends affecting this area

Once, when I was giving a speech, a young man in the audience asked, "Where do I start if I want to find out about audio-book recording?"

First, I suggested he think about what industry audio-book recording fits into—which is probably publishing—and to research it, starting there. I also asked him to consider what part of audio-book recording he might want to be involved in: editing and writing the audio, recording, providing the voice-over or what? Knowing this would help him focus his research. If he were going through this process step by step, he would be able to pinpoint that, because he already would have identified what he likes to *do* most (his most joyful skills) in Step 3.

Where does that restless gnawing in the pit of your gut fit into all this? What about the things you said you have always been attracted to?

There's no one right way to start the process of finding out more about the areas that interest you. You start in the most logical place you can think of, peel away at the information as it unfolds and follow the various paths you discover that illuminate and turn you on to ideas and sources.

What you can learn from trends

I can't emphasize enough the importance of finding out about trends. When you begin to unearth what direction an issue, entity or subject area is moving in, or what factors are driving a particular issue, you understand how you might meet a need. Trends demonstrate shifts taking place among social, cultural and economic issues. Knowing about trends can also give you an idea of where you and your skills are needed if you're clueless or fuzzy.

Trends are what help create jobs. Some jobs are created solely to solve needs as they arise or as trends shift. Ever hear of a transition champion? It's a job of the future, said human-resource specialist Richard Wilkinson, in an article at Futurist.com. This is someone who works with teams to guide them emotionally and technically as they adapt to change.

HOW TRENDS CAN AFFECT YOUR NEXT CAREER

Think about what each trend or fact means to you and what you care about. Ask:

- How will this impact the area I care about most?
- Where will there be more needs in this area?
- What's not being done to address these needs or trends?
- Is there a way to apply what I know to solve the problems related to the issues I care about?
- How could I apply my most joyful skills?
- What can I see myself actually doing?
- Is there a way to combine more than one of the areas I care about?

Companies also are creating new senior executive positions such as lead director. This is a board position that separates the chairman and chief executive jobs—most likely in reaction to the call for more intense governance in the face of corporate scandals.

As the trend toward achieving an environmentally sustainable economy in the future builds momentum, there will be more demand for such jobs as ecological economists, wind meteorologists, recycling engineers, geothermal geologists, wind turbine engineers and environmental architects, according to the World Future Society. This trend will affect other industries, including the travel industry, where eco-tourism is growing (I discuss this later in the chapter).

Some jobs are growing more than others because the problems those jobs solve are getting bigger or changing.

Look at the chiropractic field and other forms of alternative medicine. According to one study, chiropractors, practitioners of Asian medicine and naturopaths will grow by 88 percent through 2010.

What's behind this? Several trends and factors. According to the American Chiropractic Association:

1. People are more health conscious and increasingly using alternative care to address what ails them and improve overall health.
2. Chiropractic care has been shown to be a more a cost-effective treatment in comparison to surgery and other methods.
3. Chiropractic care is now included on more than 87 percent of health care plans, according to a study by the Kaiser Family Foundation. Plus, it's covered by Medicare and is available to veterans and military personnel.
4. Medical treatment is being viewed differently, with the medical doctor no longer the dictator of health but part of a team.

Accountants are another example. The need for accountants will increase as economies grow and the number of businesses increases. There will be a greater need for their services as these businesses grow, legislation changes and international competition increases.

Specifically, legislation called the Sarbanes-Oxley Act has dramatically increased the amount of work for accountants because of the requirement for more corporate governance. "Auditors must now audit and attest to the effectiveness of internal controls," explained Wayne Pinnell, managing partner of Haskell & White Certified Public Accountants and professor of accounting at California State University, Fullerton.

Other effects include an increased demand for auditors in public accounting and government positions, Big Four accounting firms and the next tier of national firms focusing their efforts on the largest companies whose projects have grown. This has created more opportunities for smaller firms to do consulting and auditing work.

Some states also are adopting legislation to bolster their corporate governance and audit requirements. And, Pinnell added, the federal government is evaluating whether to increase audit requirements for employee benefit plans, given such scandals as the one at Enron, which caused massive losses to individual retirement accounts.

The stock market and the Securities Exchange Commission "will be the ultimate drivers of accounting service growth," said Bruce Cox, partner at Callaway Partners in Atlanta. "As information for public companies is required to be filed more quickly and the penalties for inaccurate filings are increased, pressure will remain high for accounting services."

As a result of scandals, fraudulent accounting schemes and debates over ethics, Pinnell saw another trend taking shape. "The negatives seem to have created a new appeal for people to get into the profession to help restore investor confidence, investigate potential frauds and help clients through the legislative aspects."

In addition, certified management accountants (CMA) are growing in numbers. These accountants work inside corporations to help managers make financial and business decisions. They are also key players in helping companies comply with the Sarbanes-Oxley legislation, since they "are people who have the proper education to design, implement and manage internal accounting systems," said Paul Sharman, CEO of the Institute of Management Accountants, in a story at North.Jersey.com.

The demand for pastry chefs is increasing as consumers become more food savvy, more top-ranked hotels have opened and restaurants recognize the benefits of having a dedicated pastry chef, said Rowena Frith, director of the French Pastry School in Chicago. She said graduates from her school are in high demand all over, with more positions available than there are trained, experienced pastry

The fastest-growing jobs are based on demand, which is driven by trends. According to *Fast Company*, some of the fastest-growing jobs through 2012 will be:

- **Personal Financial Adviser**
  The trend: With so many people close to retirement or thinking about how much longer they need to work, people need help managing their money.
- **Medical Scientist**
  The trend: Spending on research for diseases like cancer, AIDS and Parkinson's disease is expected to increase.
- **Environmental Engineer**
  The trend: Increased environmental regulations are expected, creating strong demand for these engineers' services.
- **Post-secondary Education Administrator**
  The trend: Student enrollment is expected to increase considerably, creating a need for more of these folks.
- **Medical and Health Services Manager**
  The trend: Since the health industry is growing, it will need people to manage it.
- **Advertising and Promotions Manager**
  The trend: More world markets are continuing to open along with increased product competition.
- **Epidemiologist**
  The trend: As populations grow and barriers to travel go down, virus outbreaks will probably increase.

Seven of the top 20 jobs most likely to be in greatest demand in the next decade will call for computer expertise, according to *Fortune*. Why? For one, wireless applications are growing. Plus, the need to manage, store and search large amounts of data is huge—not to mention the crucial need to connect technologies in a secure way.

chefs. More people than ever are going to school for this specialized training. Enrollment at the French Pastry School has increased 150 percent over the last three years for its full program and 200 percent for continuing-education classes.

About 60 percent of the students are career changers, with the average age being 34 years old. Students range from lawyers, doctors, accountants and teachers to marketing and finance professionals and bus drivers. When they graduate, most will work in hotels, pastry shops, resorts or fine-dining restaurants. Others will work in food research and development, food writing, on cruise ships or will open their own businesses.

On the other hand, because of some trends, jobs will *disappear*. "Managers will become an endangered species," predicted the World Future Society in its 2005 forecast for the next 25 years. Because computers have stretched the manager's effective span of control from 6 to 21 subordinates and information flows directly from front-line workers to upper management, fewer mid-level managers will be needed, the group said.

But that trend will create other needs. Executives will have to become better prepared to deal more directly with issues that used to be handled by middle managers. Technology, of course, will play a role in supporting the executives who do that job.

What have you concluded so far?

Once you've done the research, see what you can conclude by writing:

The role or roles that sound most appealing to you:

_____

_____

_____

_____

_____

_____

What people actually do in these roles:

_____

_____

_____

_____

_____

The skills required:

_____

_____

_____

_____

_____

The kinds of organizations that might have these jobs:

_____

_____

_____

_____

_____

The environment these organizations seem to have:

_____

_____

_____

_____

_____

What the culture seems to be like:

_____

_____

_____

_____

_____

The types of people you'd interact with:

_____

_____

_____

_____

_____

Knowledge that's important to have:

_____

_____

_____

_____

_____

Experience that can be helpful:

_____

_____

_____

_____

_____

Education that can be helpful or required:

_____

_____

_____

_____

Ways to break into the field:

_____

_____

_____

_____

_____

The geographical areas jobs in this field tend to be focused in:

_____

_____

_____

_____

_____

The factors, issues or trends driving the direction this area or particular job is going in:

_____

_____

_____

_____

_____

Yes, trends matter, but

Now that you're tuned in to the importance of how trends shape industries and affect the creation of jobs, I want you also to remember what's most important about your career change: what you want.

Do not give up pursuing an avenue that's not being hailed as one of the top growing areas—if it's what you really want. You should do what you want. Not everyone changes careers to areas that are growing fields. They change to something they want to do for the love of it. The field might be hot, but that's not why they go into it.

Take these real-life examples:

- the accountant who became a belly dancer
- the teacher who started an animal sanctuary
- the documentary filmmaker who became a farmer
- the computer account manager who became a shepherd
- the ballet dancer who became an information technology manager
- the bounty hunter who became an opera singer
- the electrician who became a pilot

They all had personal reasons for pursuing these careers—even if they weren't necessarily going to be "hot" careers by someone else's standards, such as job growth, demand and salary potential.

But examining trends can open up your mind if:

▶ You're wondering, "Where are the jobs?"

▶ You're clueless or fuzzy.

▶ You want to explore how your skills, knowledge and interests match up with present and future needs of businesses, institutions and consumers.

How do you match up?

Now let's look at what you've discovered and how it fits with your new career objective. Your answers will help you see whether a field or career direction is in the zone of what you said you want.

Based on what you've discovered from your research so far, how does what you've found out match up with your new career objective? Would you be using your most joyful skills? Would you thrive in this culture and environment? Would you enjoy working with these kinds of people? Would you build on your knowledge or learn about things that interest you?

_____

_____

_____

_____

_____

_____

_____

_____

Did anything you learned make you think this isn't an area you want to continue to pursue?

_____

_____

_____

_____

_____

_____

What do you still need to know to be able to answer these questions?

_____

_____

_____

_____

_____

_____

_____

_____

_____

Evaluate your answers and compare them to your new career objective by taking out a blank sheet of paper, creating two columns and filling in this information:

What I discovered about the area(s) I care about	What I want
Main skills I might use:	My most joyful skills:
Environment and culture seem to be:	Environment and culture I thrive in:
People I might work with:	My favorite people to work with:
Required or useful knowledge:	I'm interested in knowing and learning more about:

How does what you discovered match up with what you want?

Here are some other examples of trends and issues—some of which I have combined into more than one area of interest.

WOMEN/CONSUMERS

According to *Road & Travel*:

- Women are a dominant force in business and purchasing power, making up 83 percent of all consumer purchases, said Marty Barletta in her book *Marketing To Women*.

- This includes 94 percent of home furnishings, 92 percent of vacations, 91 percent of houses, 51 percent of consumer electronics, 60 percent of cars, 89 percent of new bank accounts, 80 percent of decisions about health care and two thirds of all health care spending.

- Women comprise 40 percent of business travel.

- When it comes to the aftermarket, women make up 65 percent of the customer base for service centers. Eighty percent feel dissatisfied with the service and repairs they receive and 89 percent feel they're treated differently because of their gender.

- Women take more all-female adventure tours than ever before. To meet this need, companies are specializing in adventure travel and women-only tours or trips that focus on shopping or spirituality pilgrimages and retreats. According to a *New York Times* article, these tours can emphasize the chance to surf, climb mountains or sail in all-female groups or a trip that includes daily massages and a creative-writing trip to South Carolina.

- Women-only spas are a growing trend.

- An estimated 10.6 million privately held firms in the United States were 50 percent or more female owned, accounting for 48 percent of all privately held businesses in 2004, said Leslie Grossman, co-founder of Women's Leadership Exchange. These companies generate $2.45 trillion in sales and employ 19.1 million people.

AGING/HEALTH

According to the U.S. Census Bureau and the World Health Organization:

▸ People are living longer than ever before, with the average life expectancy in developed countries ranging from 76 to 80 years. In the United States, the number of people aged 65 is expected to increase from 35 million in 2000 to an estimated 71 million in 2030. The number of people aged 80 years is expected to increase from 9.3 million in 2000 to 19.5 million in 2030.

▸ The leading causes of death have gone from infectious disease and acute illness to chronic disease and degenerative illness.

▸ In the United States, approximately 80 percent of people aged 65 years have at least one chronic condition and 50 percent have at least two. Diabetes affects approximately one in five people over 65, and as the population ages, the impact of diabetes will intensify.

▸ As people live longer, Alzheimer's disease will become more prevalent. Approximately 10 percent of people aged 65 and 47 percent aged 85 suffer from this disease. Arthritis affects about 59 percent of people aged 65 years.

▸ All of these trends create more demands for long-term care and greater challenges for individuals and families. This will put increased demands on the public-health system as well as medical and social services.

▸ A major health care trend is to help older people live independently. Businesses that do this include those offering nonmedical home care with hourly or live-in care, meal preparation, medication reminders and transportation. Others help seniors deal with paperwork, teach computer skills or offer online dating services.

▸ With the growing elderly population, there will be a greater need for social workers to meet their needs for mental and physical health care, living arrangements and dealing with end-of-life and aging issues. According to the National Association of Social Workers, the lack of social workers to meet these needs could be significant. Studies find that almost 30 percent of social workers today are over the age of 55. This trend will also affect the ability to deliver social services for other adults, children and families dealing with things such as natural and other disasters, poverty, disease, violence and child welfare.

HEALTH/FITNESS

The United States is full of people increasingly looking to alternative medicine. One trend is toward simplifying the fitness experience.

Health clubs belonging to the International Health, Racquet & Sportsclub Association reported that 4.5 million members were under the age of 18 in 2002, according to the Associated Press.

One third of all U.S. teenagers are inactive; only 32 percent of kids age 6–17 meet minimum standards for cardiovascular fitness, flexibility, muscular strength and endurance; 40 percent of first-graders have at least one coronary disease risk factor, according to Fitwize4kids on Springwise.com.

Up to 80 percent of the U.S. male population doesn't work out on a regular basis, said Springwise.com.

About 18 million adults are obese and another 137 million are overweight, according to a study published in 2005 in *The Lancet. The New England Journal of Medicine* cited another report saying that in developing countries, "as many as 60 percent of households with an underweight family member also have an overweight one."

CONSUMERISM

Statistics about America's spending show that income has increased, leading to more consumption and changing priorities. For example, consumers are spending less on food and more on dining out, according to AdAge.com.

The most surprising trend that Mechele Flaum, president of BrainReserve, has encountered is what she calls "atmos fear," which is "consumers' wariness about the environment, food sources, plane rides, etc.," according to *Crain's*

New York Business. Consumers are also concerned about how companies conduct business and how they treat their employees. She refers to this as "vigilante consumerism."

▶ There is a shift in the way we shop, with the growth of smaller shopping centers with a "Main Street" feel and the boom in e-commerce, said Paco Underhill, author of *Why We Buy* on RetailIndustry.com.

▶ Spending on pet products has more than doubled in the last decade, according to the American Pet Products Manufacturer's Association, with the U.S. Census Bureau ranking the pet industry as the seventh-largest retail segment in the United States.

ECONOMICS/ENVIRONMENT

▶ There is a trend toward creating a sustainable "eco-economy" that meets the needs of future generations, according to the World Future Society. This will mean investments in such areas as fish farming, wind-farm construction and turbine manufacturing, hydrogen generation, fuel-cell and solar-cell manufacturing, light-rail construction, bicycle manufacturing and tree planting.

▶ Ecotourism is catching on. Defined by The International Ecotourism Society as "responsible travel to natural areas that conserves the environment and improves the well-being of local people," resorts and "eco-lodges" that preserve and minimize impact on the environment are popping up as new travel destinations. An example is Blancaneaux Lodge in Belize, which is "designed not to leave a huge footprint on the environment," wrote Michelle Greene in an article in *The New York Times* in 2005. Ninety percent of the lodge's power comes from a hydroelectric plant, and the garden and citrus orchards are organic.

FAMILY

▶ A revolution is in full swing via a cultural splintering that erases lines and "shoulds," wrote Hallmark's trend expert Marita Wesely-Clough in an article at RetailIndustry.com. Singles outnumber couples, legislators and courts are redefining marriage, oldsters are living together, older children are living at home, there's an acceptance of family planning via adoption, science or surrogates and friends are like family. "Watch for a rapid evolution in the way families take shape and new communities take root and thrive, possibly resulting in dramatic effects on social, political, medical and economic infrastructures."

▶ Priorities are shifting as people want to work less and spend more time with family.

▶ The U.S. Census Bureau figures for 2003 show one third of men and nearly one quarter of women between 30 and 34 have never been married, according to a 2005 Associated Press article.

FOOD

According to the Food Channel Trendwire:

▶ Family dining is in. The slow-food movement will encourage families to spend more time eating together at home, said Robin Kline, a food industry consultant.

▶ More restaurants and cafes will offer no-carb, low-carb, gluten-free and vegetarian entrées on their menus.

▶ Growing demand for organic farm foods will boost the popularity of goat and sheep cheeses.

▶ As we hear more about gastric-bypass surgery, a new Gastric Bypass Diet may be spawned, said food journalist Marge Perry.

ENERGY/CLIMATE

▶ Some 42,000 new jobs will be created in the solar industry by 2015, according to the Solar Energy Industries Association. The driving force is the looming natural-gas crisis.

▶ There is a concerted effort around the world to do a better job of predicting climate. Climateprediction.net is one project working to do that, offering a model for global networking and collaboration and ways to tackle such issues as water resources and energy demand.

TECHNOLOGY/BEAUTY

With so much concern about looks and health, one company is developing a digital visualization of what junk food, excess alcohol and lack of exercise will do to your looks, according to *The New Scientist*. French laboratory Accenture Technology is working on a system that captures and displays your image by wireless camera with a computer that builds a profile of your lifestyle. It shows you what you can expect to look like in the future if you continue with your current eating, drinking and exercise habits.

ENGINEERING

According to a 2004 article in the *Mississippi Business Journal*:

▶ Computer security and computer forensics are two big, emerging fields of engineering, said Dr. Bob Taylor of Mississippi State University, with the emphasis on becoming a resource to help train law enforcement agents.

▶ Aerospace and biological engineering are growing, with engineers involved in medical fields doing such things as designing devices and implants and growing tissue for burn victims.

▶ Demand for environmental engineers will increase by more than 54 percent during the next 10 years, said *Fortune*, because of an increasingly health-conscious public that's eager to prevent environmental problems instead of just controlling the problems that exist.

LANGUAGE

▶ The greatest need for bilingual employees in the United States is in the consumer-services sector in such areas as banking, retail and telecommunications, said the Society for Human Resource Management. Bilingual medical and legal administrative staff also is needed.

▶ The top 10 foreign languages spoken in the world are Mandarin Chinese, Hindi, Spanish, English, Bengali, Portuguese, Russian, Japanese, German and Korean, according to the *World Almanac*.

▶ Chile has begun a sweeping effort to make the country bilingual, with the long-term goal being to make all 15 million of its people fluent in English within a generation, stated a 2004 article in the *New York Times*. Chileans are linked more than ever to an international presence. "If you can't speak English, you can't sell and you can't learn," said the minister of education. Besides teaching elementary and high-school students, the government is trying to reach adults by encouraging businesses to offer English courses to employees. Government officials say their biggest problem is a lack of qualified teachers.

▶ With blogs ("Web logs," or Web journals) becoming so popular, bloggers "swarm around a new piece of information; push, prod, and poke at it; and leave it either stronger or a bloody mess," observed *Fortune* in January 2005. This has led to the creation of companies that watch the Web for corporate customers and provide warnings of impending catastrophes. Blogging publishers also are emerging.

LAW

▶ Technology will continue to impact the practice of law, with research and brief-writing being done online with computers activated and manipulated by voice commands, said Glen Hiemstra, a future consultant, in an article at Futurist.com.

▶ Hiemstra also said that because of technology—including biotechnology—lawyers will grapple with issues related to privacy rights and ethics. Telemedicine is raising issues of patient privacy, professional liability and practicing medicine in other states besides the one where a doctor's license was issued. Also, interstate bank branching will have expanded to international branching and the World Court Concept will be a reality, with international disputes presented at international tribunals.

EDUCATION

According to *The Futurist*:

▶ Teachers complain about being battered and intimidated, administrators feel unappreciated, school boards get criticized for micromanaging and students are being tested to death.

Four factors are driving educational change: decentralization and educational options, performance evaluation and success measurement, changes in leadership and leadership roles and reconfigurations of learning spaces.

Busy parents may hire parent surrogates to help their children be effective learners.

More and more, teachers will be at the center of administration, instruction and evaluation.

Machines—computers and/or other technology—will probably replace teachers in the future to provide instruction. But among the obstacles that continue to keep technology out of the classroom for the immediate future are teachers' fears of and objections to technology.

After the 2004 tragedy in Beslan, Russia, in which a school was held hostage and adults and children were killed, many families from Russia, Belarus, Estonia, Lithuania, and Ukraine inquired about U.S. home-school curricula. This reaction mirrors what happens in the United States after an incidence of school violence. Author John C. Lundt said home schooling might be part of a larger trend toward "learning without schools."

PROJECT MANAGEMENT

As businesses, government and nonprofit organizations focus more on quality, cost control, getting things done quickly and standardizing tasks, the need for project management has grown.

Project management has "emerged as a premier solution in business operations," said Larry Richman, author of *Project Management Step-By-Step*. "Large and small organizations recognize that structured approach to planning and controlling projects is a necessary core competency for success."

Many organizations and universities offer professional development such as the Project Management Institute and the International Project Management Association. They provide certification, degrees, seminars and networking opportunities.

> Project managers work in construction, engineering, architecture, manufacturing, real estate development and information technology, said WetFeet, a source for career information.

SECURITY

As issues such as privacy, terrorism and overall rage in society become more prominent, security will continue to grow. Security covers issues such as cyberspace, immigration and borders, security preparedness and response, biological and chemical emergencies and disasters, hazardous devices, travel and transportation, infrastructure protection, threats and food safety.

> Security encompasses such professions as guards, police, detectives, investigators, special agents, bodyguards and correctional officers.

> Computer security is one of the top priorities of companies and their information-technology managers, as white-collar criminals and hackers are on the prowl and computer fraud and software piracy continue to be issues.

> The view that anti-U.S. terrorism is linked to U.S. foreign policy and not to some vague hatred of freedom will gain momentum, said Glen Hiemstra, a speaker on the future.

> Future terrorist attacks may occur in rural areas, a U.S. Department of Homeland Security report concluded.

> The surveillance camera market has swelled to nearly $6 billion and will grow at 25 percent per year, said security analyst Scott Greiper in a 2005 Reuters article, with Americans becoming increasingly tolerant of having their movements recorded. Net earnings for thermal night-vision camera maker Flir Systems increased more than 60 percent in 2004. With the Homeland Security budget growing, President Bush requested $600 million for the Targeted Infrastructure Protection program.

> "Surveillance devices aimed at humans are proliferating at an unprecedented rate, from lasers that can monitor members of a crowd for abnormal vital signs to biometric

scanners that pick out individual travelers at a distance and link them to vast commercial and government databases containing their detailed personal information," said a January 2005 story in *Fortune*. The article added that the Central Intelligence Agency has been funding ways to spy on Internet chat rooms.

▶ Besides terrorist fears, the surge in road rage, high-profile school shootings and the perception of an increase in crime are causing many to call for increased video surveillance, the Electronic Privacy Information Center stated on its Web site.

Activity 3: Brain-tapping (others)

In a 2005 article in the *New York Times Magazine*, Charles McGrath described a theory held by writer Tom Wolfe. He calls it "information compulsion," which is that "most people are dying to tell you something you don't know, whether they're surfers, strippers, astronauts, car customizers."

People do love to give advice and tell you what they know. Take advantage of it in this next activity by doing just that—tapping the brains of live human beings. You'll not only find out what they know, but you can prove or disprove what you discovered and find out what you didn't learn from your research so far. People will also be able to give you the type of information only someone close to the field would know, which will help you look at reality—something you need to do quite closely in this process.

In their book, *Confronting Reality: Doing What Matters to Get Things Right*, authors Larry Bossidy and Ram Charan advised businesses on how to succeed. It's great advice for you too. They said the greatest damage to businesses and owners is the failure to confront reality. One of the easiest ways to avoid the problem is to talk. "Mostly you need to converse," they wrote. "What could be simpler? Yet we see so many people who don't do it—that is, they don't do it proactively, by asking questions, listening and keeping their minds open about the answers."

This next activity is about asking questions, listening and keeping an open mind about what you learn.

WHO TO TALK TO

Talk to two categories of people:

1. People you already know who could either:

    a. Give you input on your areas of interest, or
    b. Refer you to someone to get input on your areas of interest

If the people you know don't work directly in the area you're interested in, they should have knowledge of it. They could have once worked in this area or dabbled in it. If, for instance, you're interested in learning more about political jobs, find someone who ran for a political office. Maybe they're on the city council or work in a government job. They could work for a company that's highly regulated and be in a role that's closely aligned with lobbyists or has political agendas.

Look around at who you know from various parts of your life— relatives, friends, fellow committee members or people who attend your place of worship.

Who do you know who might have ties to or knowledge of your areas of interest? Think about professionals you deal with—lawyers, accountants, doctors, chiropractors, business people, brokers and who they might know and refer you to. Don't assume they don't know anyone who can help you. They all have friends, neighbors and relatives too.

The best way to approach your acquaintances is to share your objective and ask if they'll give you input or refer you to people who can. In a minute, I'll get more specific on how to explain to people what you're doing.

2. Specific people or types of people you want to talk to but don't know

They can include folks you have read about in your research, learned of or know of in some other way. If, for instance, you're interested in alternative health care, the person might be a local authority in the field of holistic health or education who you saw quoted in an article in the newspaper. They might have written a book about the area you're interested in.

You can approach these people with letters, phone calls or e-mails explaining your objective and asking for a half hour of their time. You could also ask people in the first group if they know this person and ask to be referred.

When my client Beth, the engineer, got to this part of the process, she didn't have a specific person she wanted to talk to, but she did have a particular type in mind: people who work in the field of industrial design. She found them by attending a meeting of the local chapter of industrial designers.

DON'T BE FOOLED

I offer two cautions as you research and talk to people:

1. **Don't jump to conclusions too fast. Sometimes it's best to ponder the information you've obtained.**
   One of my clients, who one week was gung ho about getting into pharmaceuticals sales, told me a week later, "No way!" Why? Someone told her that these sales representatives get no respect. Every time she heard a piece of information, she took it as gospel. She bounced back and forth, never taking my advice to check something out further and as a result, had trouble getting anywhere. So, listen to what people say, put it in the "That's Interesting" pile and check it out more.

2. **Get more than one perspective.**
   One person in an industrial-design firm told Beth she'd have to go back to school to work in a firm like his—even as an account manager—since the best account managers were designers first. At least two other people told her the opposite.
   After talking to a wide range of people, she came away from all of these discussions clearer on her options and confident that there is a role for her. She became focused on where to go next.

Another client, Phillip, a lawyer, was in the beginning stages of figuring out how he could work in the areas he cared most about: food and special events. After doing his initial research, he decided he wanted to know more about meeting and event planning and possibly owning a restaurant. He didn't know anyone in meeting and event planning. But through his research, he discovered a company that offered a meeting-planning "boot camp." He contacted this company to get the inside scoop on the industry.

My client Jerry, the operations analyst and sales associate, had read a personal trainer's book on weightlifting that had made an impact on him. Jerry decided to write him to get his thoughts on wellness.

How to kick off the conversation

When Beth, the engineer, was at the point of talking to people, she started by delivering a 30-second introduction that included key points of the new objective she had developed. She told people:

> *"I am exploring how to capitalize on my engineering background and passion for incorporating technology into innovative new products. I have spent 12 years honing my strengths. These are my ability to research and analyze the design and usability of new products and my ability to communicate effectively with engineers, designers and customers and solve problems related to functionality. One area that I'm looking at is industrial design. I'm not necessarily looking at becoming a designer, but I'm exploring, perhaps, a liaison role between the client and designer."*

You also want to be ready to elaborate on your background.

What to ask

Once you're ready to talk to people, look for insight into the area or areas you've researched on your own thus far. You want to know what it's like, where you might fit in, what the trends are, what education is required—anything to help you know whether you want to pursue it and in what direction to dig further.

Start by looking at what you wrote in answer to the last question in Activity 2, when you were assessing how you matched up: *What do you still need to know to be able to assess if you match up to this type of career?* Write out specific questions you want to ask someone based on this.

Look at what you wrote in answer to this question from Activity 2 when you were assessing how you matched up: *Did anything you learned make you think this wasn't an area to continue to pursue?* If so, ask for more input before you negate the idea.

Also, in general, what do you still want to know that you didn't learn from your research? Write down your answer. Other questions you might ask people include:

- What social, economic, political, environmental, cultural and technological forces influence this area?
- What does it take to get into this field or profession?
- What do you like about it? What do you dislike about it?
- What's an ideal background?
- What's a typical day like?
- What education do you need?
- How much does experience count?
- Can you see someone like me fitting in? If so, where?
- What obstacles might I run into? How could I overcome them?

Let's say you are interested in the delivery of health care. After doing your research—not to mention having your own personal experience—you conclude that one of the biggest issues in health care today is that there are more patients, and physicians have limited time to spend with those patients. This problem will only increase as the population ages. As one 20-something told me when I asked him why he was interested in medicine, "A lot of people are getting old."

Either by talking to someone or through your reading—or again, through personal experience—you'll no doubt stumble upon the field of physician's assistant. Working under the supervision of a physician, the assistant takes medical histories, examines and treats patients, orders and interprets lab tests and X-rays, diagnoses and prescribes medications.

According to the U.S. Department of Labor's Bureau of Labor Statistics, this field is expected to grow faster than the average for all occupations through 2012. What's behind this? The anticipated expansion of the health services industry and emphasis on cost containment.

You can generate more conversation on this by sharing what you've discovered in your research. For example, if you're interested in health care but not sure where you'd fit in, you could say: "Based on my personal experience with doctors' offices and the growing expansion of health services and emphasis on cost containment, I understand it's becoming more common for doctors to have physician's assistants and medical assistants. Can you tell me more about that?"

If you're really hazy about where you'd fit into this area you're researching, start with an open-ended question such as, "What are the possible ways to be involved in this area?" As the person talks, ask more about what sounds most appealing to you, and drill down to get more data, such as what skills are required, what it takes to get into that field and what trends are affecting the growth of that area.

If you are interested in nursing but unsure about education, you can ask the person to clear up your confusion. Do you need a four-year degree, an associate's degree or other diploma? What if you already have a degree—is there an accelerated study program? Much of this you can learn in your research phase. But you might ask about the best schools or Web sites that can help. Check with the American Association of Colleges of Nursing (www.aacn.nche.edu) and nursesource.org for additional information.

ONLINE CONVERSATIONS

You also can "talk" to people online, by utilizing chat rooms, news groups or message boards.

For example, search engines such as Google and Yahoo allow you to start your own group or online community of like-minded people where you share information and ask questions. Browse existing groups on these engines, including those that discuss arts and entertainment, computers, recreation, science and technology, business and finance, health, society and humanities.

You can set up an alert with these search engines that will sift through 4,500 news sources from around the world and then send you articles related to your subject area as they are published. This keeps you updated on trends and gives you potential sources of information to tap.

But don't rely solely on online data. As Columbia University graduate School of Journalism professor Sree Sreenifasan said, "Google

> Does the world have a need for what you think you want to do? How do you know? What trends, issues, causes and problems exist that can use you? How will what you do make a difference?

> What specific organizations deal with the issues or problems that concern you? Or might you deal with them on your own?

> Which organizations would you want to work for?

> What's the future potential for this work? Where is it headed? What other problems might it address?

> Where does your "gnawing" fit in?

is a place for clues—not answers." You will still need to talk to humans and conduct more research.

What have you discovered and concluded?

After talking to people, what did you learn? Does what you learned match up with what you thought and gathered from your research? Did you learn anything that makes you want to eliminate a particular role? Does it make sense to pursue this direction, area or particular job? How does it match up with what you said you want in your new career objective?

When Beth was exploring industrial design, she spoke to her father (an engineer at an industrial design firm), college professors, designers and sales people who worked in these firms, two friends from college who worked at manufacturers and an executive at a manufacturer. She even attended an out-of-town trade show where industrial designers were meeting. She met people from companies she was interested in working for, which helped her later in the marketing phase.

In her research phase and through her discussions, she discovered and concluded that:

- The industry is small.
- People might perceive her as a "tech head."
- She wanted to focus her energy on companies making products that excite her.
- A number of companies make products she likes within a 500-mile radius of where she lives, giving her insight into whom to possibly target.
- She was certain she didn't want to be an industrial designer because she didn't want to draw and render.
- She didn't want to be an account manager in an industrial-design firm.
- She wanted to be in a liaison role where she would track emerging technology and help determine how that could be applied to a company's products.
- There actually is a role that sounded perfect for her skills, interests and knowledge: a technology watchdog for a manufacturer.

Phillip, my client who was researching meeting and event planning and possibly owning a restaurant, talked to several restaurant owners and concluded that he did not want to pursue owning a restaurant at this time. The long hours didn't fit the immediate future he envisioned for himself that he defined in Step 4 and the initial capital investment was too high. He concluded that meeting and event planning better matched his career objective and personal values.

Even Robert F. Kennedy, son of Robert Kennedy, did his homework when it came to contemplating a change. He spent weeks holding meetings with politicians throughout the state of New York and consulting Kennedy family members before making up his mind on whether to run for state attorney general, according to the *New York Times*.

Getting a variety of opinions also makes a difference. After talking with his wife, kids, uncle, brothers and sisters, Kennedy said, "It's funny. All the family members who had not been in political office urged me to run and the ones who had served in office urged me not to."

In early 2005, he announced that he had decided against it, concluding that to run a successful campaign, he would have too little time with his wife and six children. He was unwilling to make that sacrifice.

After my client Jerry, the operations analyst and sales associate, went through this three-step process researching his key areas of interest—healthy lifestyles, wellness and education—he discovered statistics and data such as these:

▶ Americans are fatter than ever, with nearly two thirds of adults 20 to 74 years old and about one in six young persons classified as overweight, according to the Center for Disease Control.

▶ More than 77 percent of U.S. adults believe that childhood obesity is a major problem and that the rising rate of childhood obesity is a public health problem and an issue of personal responsibility, according to results from a Harris Interactive poll posted on WSJ.com.

▶ The U.S. life expectancy is predicted to decline later in this century, say researchers at the University of Illinois at Chicago in a report from the *New England Journal of Medicine*. They based their predictions on the dramatic rise in obesity—especially among young people and minorities. They say obesity will shorten the average life span of 77.6 years by at least two to five years.

▶ Congress is subjecting food companies to more scrutiny, as concerns increase over elevated obesity rates and diet-related illnesses, according to the *New York Times*. To respond, some companies are creating "heath and wellness" initiatives and "putting people who might otherwise be critics on the payroll."

From his conversations with people, he confirmed that:

- People are looking for others who are able to help them evaluate their health.
- Overall, the average American is in a sorry state of personal health, with a strong correlation between being healthy and being happy.
- People don't notice how problems in their lives might be connected to their daily habits—for example, getting headaches because of not drinking enough water, or feeling moody because of a vitamin B deficiency.

SIX SUPERTRENDS SHAPING THE FUTURE

Edward Cornish, author of *Futuring: The Exploration of the Future*, said there are six "supertrends" that summarize a key category of change and act as a key force in human life today:

▶ **Technological progress**
This includes all the improvements being made in computers, medicine, transportation and other technologies that enable us to achieve our purposes more effectively.

▶ **Economic growth**
The first trend promotes this one because people are eager to use their know-how to produce goods and services to use and sell.

▶ **Improving health**
The first two have led to this and this leads to increasing longevity, which, Cornish said, has two important consequences: population growth and a rise in the average age.

▶ **Increasing mobility**
This is the ability for people, goods and information to move from place to place faster and in greater quantity than ever before.

▶ **Environment decline**
Continuing high population growth and economic development are creating this, which has led to Mother Earth becoming sick and getting sicker.

▶ **Loss of traditional culture**
This is due to such factors as high mobility, rapid change and economic growth.

He also came across an article at RetailIndustry.com citing one of Faith Popcorn's 2003 forecasts, which said that as people grapple with eating habits, a new vocation will emerge—the food coach.

Although "food coach" didn't describe fully what he thought he wanted to do, it helped Jerry see the need for one part of what he could do. He was pumped after getting feedback and seeing how much potential interest and need existed for what he cared about most.

After all the input he got, he concluded, "I want to help people who have started to think about how to improve their health, or tried in the past, be happier by helping them come up with diet, exercise, sleep- and stress-management behaviors and attitudes right for them—as opposed to cramming their needs into an off-the-shelf diet or exercise program.

"That means that I want to explore how to be someone who acts as a personal trainer and diet consultant who gives guidance and motivation on nutrition, exercise, relaxation and sleep."

In this role, he could see himself fulfilling his new career objective, which was having a career where he would be:

- *Using his most joyful skills*: assessing, advising, motivating, communicating, creating visuals and counseling
- *Working with people he defined as those he would most enjoy being around*: self-motivated people who are unhappy with the way they look and feel
- *Incorporating his knowledge about*: diet, nutrition, exercise, nutrition, stress management, working with the public, small-business development and operations and marketing
- *Applying what he cared most about*: healthy lifestyles, wellness and education

Exactly where he would do this and precisely what he'd be called was yet to be determined. But he knew he wanted to be in an environment and culture where he would thrive—which would challenge him to always get better, reward him for doing a good job and give him respectful feedback. He was anxious to give it a name, but for the time being, he focused on what he might do and why someone would pay him for his services.

That brings us to the last thing you need to do before moving to the next step.

Develop your Why the World Would Care Statement

If you cannot explain how someone would benefit from what you want to do, it will be hard to create a career around it and get others to want to hire you or buy what you have to offer. So now you have to think about how your work would make a difference to someone else.

Think about it in this way: What would contributing your most joyful skills, knowledge, passion and interests to your potential intended audience or entity lead to? What would it result in? Why would anyone care if you did it? Are you making something safer, disseminating important information or making someone's life better?

SAMPLE WHY THE WORLD WOULD CARE STATEMENTS:

I would improve the health and well-being of others.

I would develop business processes that create efficiency and continuous improvement in sales and marketing, operations and investment strategies.

I would prevent environmental problems and care for our resources for the future of our children and our planet.

I would establish internal controls and procedures that assure legal and fiscal compliance and sound, strategic decisions for financial professionals.

I would make sure all projects are completed on time and within budget.

I'd develop code and programming that leads to efficient business processes and practices.

I would improve aesthetics, design and functionality of everyday, technological products.

I would make people's lives safer.

I would transport people to another place, where they could laugh and cry and think about things they might not have thought about before.

I would safeguard people's privacy.

I would improve the efficacy of new drugs.

I would deliver memorable travel and meeting experiences for people.

Complete this statement:

The world would care about what I can do because:

_____

_____

_____

_____

_____

_____

_____

_____

_____

_____

Now, you are ready to add this statement to your new Career Objective. Using all four parts of your career objective and your Why the World Would Care Statement, write your new Complete Career Objective:

_____

_____

_____

_____

_____

_____

_____

_____

_____

_____

_____

_____

_____

Sample new Complete Career Objective:

▶ I'd assess, advise, motivate, communicate with, create visuals for and counsel . . .

▶ self-motivated people who are unhappy with the way they look and feel . . .

▶ where I'd be trusted to do a good job, challenged to always get better, rewarded for doing a good job and receive respectful feedback . . .

▶ incorporating my knowledge about diet, nutrition, exercise, stress management, working with the public, small-business development and operations and marketing . . .

▶ by applying my passion for or interest in healthy lifestyles, wellness and education.

▶ This work would lead to improving the health and well-being of others (the Why the World Would Care Statement).

Now you're ready to explore what it might take to pursue your new objective and how willing you are to go after it.

Your exact steps will vary

In this chapter I have given you three key activities to do to explore where you might fit into the world. These activities will help you get and test ideas and further define your next career. Although I've listed these steps in a precise order, how you execute them will depend on how much you know about what you want to do next and how you think.

When people work with me as their coach, each step and activity I take them through and the order in which we do it depends on how clear, creative and open-minded they are, and how they feel, overall, about their life. Sometimes I don't go in the exact order I've listed here. I might pose questions to one person I wouldn't think of asking someone else.

Patty, for example, came to me at age 66 to evaluate her strengths and value and how to continue to have a career within the parameters she had defined at that point in her life. She had owned her own small business for 15 years, and was now working in sales for the new owner. It would have been acceptable to her to keep doing that job, but she wasn't thrilled with the company's direction. In addition, something else was nudging at her.

At the end of our third meeting, she was vacillating about whether to stay where she was—in a comfortable, familiar situation—or explore this feeling. She told me, "If I don't do something with this thought, there will always be a nag about whether I missed an opportunity, and I will wonder if I could have done it." So, onward we explored.

She was taking art classes and volunteering at a small museum where she immersed herself in things she loved—architecture, culture, art, beautiful fabrics and history. She also loved to travel, and had planned walking and bicycle tours during trips she and her family had taken to other countries.

Her most joyful skills included communicating, presenting, persuading, training, motivating and developing relationships.

Her knowledge—from work and life experience—was in three key areas: small-business operations, interior design and textiles, and art and architecture.

IF YOU'RE CLUELESS

▸ Look at the list of issues and problems the world deals with. Which areas interest you?

▸ Which ones do you care about most? Which issues are you drawn to or have you been involved in during your life?

▸ Which trends are affecting that issue or area?

▸ How do you want to affect those? What difference would you like to make?

▸ What skills do you have to do that?

ENTREPRENEURIAL TYPES BUILD ON TRENDS

Faith Popcorn introduced the trend of cocooning in the 1990s and it's still gaining momentum. If you're the entrepreneurial type, this is a good example of how to take advantage of the direction in which things are moving.

Cocooning is the behavior people exhibit when they insulate themselves from normal social environments. She suggests that cocooning can fall into three areas: where someone retreats to the privacy of their home, when someone creates a barrier to protect themselves from external threats or when someone travels with technological barriers that insulate them from the environment.

Take advantage of this trend by creating a "house call" option for whatever you do, suggests life coach Soni Pitts. Bring your service or product—that people normally would have to go out to buy—to them.

Another trend is the consumption of wine. In 2003, table-wine consumption in the United States hit an all-time high of 232 million cases consumed, according to the Wine Market Council.

Let's say you're interested in wine. It's something you collect or discuss. Building on the trend, how could you turn your love of this drink of the gods into a career? Don't just think winery or retail store. Look at other trends that Americans have developed for all things wine related. Think about how you could create a business or be involved in one that's peripheral to wineries. Some people have entered this market as wine educators, wine game inventors, wine accessory manufacturers and builders who design cellars, according to Entrepreneur.com.

When one existing company looked around and noticed the number of enthusiastic but underinformed wine lovers, the Traveling

Vineyard became their home-based business arm. Geerlings & Wade, a marketer of wine and wine accessories, now offers people the chance to host wine-tasting parties (they're like Tupperware parties for wine) through the help of their Independent Personal Wine Consultants, said Springwise.com.

So, if you want to get involved, write down everything you can think of related to wine. Visit stores, read wine magazines and talk to wine experts at your local stores. If you're a wine connoisseur, what do you want that doesn't exist? Based on your skills and interests and what consumers want, what could you do to meet that need?

If getting healthy and fit is what gets your juices flowing, you might consider creating a career around niche health and fitness—another growing trend.

The more specific you can be in the service you offer, the better. Even better: Simplify the fitness experience offering, for example, brief workouts to women and health and fitness programs targeted at kids and families.

Again, think about ancillary products or services related to this industry and your strongest skills. Could you see yourself consulting, educating, writing or managing something that has to do with health and fitness?

Another trend is serving the senior market. There are businesses that offer nonmedical home care, for instance. This can include hourly or live-in care providing meal preparation, medication reminders and transportation.

I know a woman who created a business that focuses solely on helping seniors deal with paperwork related to medical insurance. Other businesses prepare and deliver meals and teach computer skills to seniors, while another offers an online dating service. If you're in this demographic or have senior family members, what do they need that no one offers?

Are you the entrepreneurial type?

Entrepreneurs realize when there's a need, and they take advantage of the opportunity. If you apply that same mindset to your career, you can sniff out jobs—even create them. But some people want to do their own thing. If you're thinking of going out on your own, here are some of the qualities and characteristics it takes:

▶ **You feel comfortable taking risks.**

▶ **You can live with uncertainty and ambiguity.**

▶ **You like to take charge of something and see it through.**

▶ **You plan.**

▶ **You don't mind working hard and sticking with something, even when things get in the way.**

▶ **You have the courage to make decisions.**

▶ **You have a lot of self-discipline.**

▶ **You're creative and come up with new approaches and ideas.**

▶ **You get excited about creating products or services.**

▶ **You have a sense of what people want and how to get it to them.**

She was intrigued and cared most about two main areas: a) travel and everything associated with it, including architecture, art, culture and food, and b) the mind/body connection to health and stress.

She envisioned a life in which she worked but had the flexibility to volunteer, travel, exercise and enjoy what she called "quiet time."

In her work, she wanted to have an impact on the world by promoting something she was excited about and by motivating others to be involved with it or have access to it. She saw herself doing this by, as she put it, "being a connector between someone who wanted to know more about something and that product or service."

Although I didn't want her to focus on job titles for herself, as a way to start thinking about this, I asked her to brainstorm about these kinds of activities and where they take place out in the world. She was conceptual enough to understand. I wouldn't do this with everyone.

So, I asked her, "Who might do that? Who might be a liaison between someone and information that someone wants in the areas you know and care about?" It simply seemed like the right question to ask her at that moment.

Being a creative and open person, Patty came up with all kinds of ideas. They included an art, fabric or accessory representative for home décor or lighting; a travel agent or tour guide; or someone who promotes the services of a health care facility or educational entity or conference.

Again, we weren't evaluating whether these were jobs she wanted, just throwing out ideas to get her thinking. As she talked, I tossed out more questions: Is there a way to combine your interest in health and stress with the travel? Keeping in mind your vision for how you want your life, what package might this come in? This got us talking about whether this would be something she would do on her own or for someone else.

She was wise enough to understand what she *didn't* know. And our brainstorming and questioning led us to come up with information she wanted to research and questions she wanted to ask people in the travel and health care industries.

Step 8

Know what it will cost you.

You've done your soul-searching, blue-skying, what-iffing and analyzing, and you've got your new career objective based on who you are—not what others think you should be. And now that you've explored trends and issues, you have some ideas on where you'd fit in.

It's time to bring all that back to earth and deal with other concerns that have been nagging at you—like how you're going to make this new career happen.

First, though, you need to face a moment of reckoning.

Based on what you've discovered so far about what you want to go after, *do you really want this?*

Does it feel like the right thing to pursue? Even if you don't have an exact title to call yourself—even though you don't know how much this new direction is going to pay or precisely where you'll do it—does your heart tell you that everything you've figured out so far feels right? Even if you may be inconvenienced, uncomfortable, even scared at times, do you want this change enough?

If you said yes—I know in my heart it's the right thing to pursue and I have made the choice to do that—write this down and post it in a place you see every day: "I know in my heart this is the right thing to do."

You'll need your heart to anchor you because there is plenty other stuff that will try to pull you away from it, which we'll get into in a minute.

Assuming you said yes, the question is now, *How much will it cost you to get to the next step and go after what you want?*

> *"Follow your heart.*
> *It's the one organ that will surely let you down one day,*
> *so don't waste it while you're living."*
>
> NIMIAN, a character in the movie *The Road To Wellness*

By that, I don't just mean money. I mean, what will it cost you in terms of time, relationships, risk, inconvenience and money? Specifically, these kinds of things:

1. How much time will you need to invest in this?
2. What will you have to give up? Your job, time with family, vacations, Starbucks, massages, manicures, a feeling of security?
3. Will it cost you money? If so, how much and for what? Education? Living off of savings? Getting professional assistance as you go to the next step?
4. Who will you have to persuade to get on board and support you while you make the change?
5. Who might you need to cut ties or reconcile differences with about your career path and life?
6. What part of your ego needs to take a backseat?

You're at the place where you need to examine and confront these real-life issues. Put another way, we're ready to look at how you will need to change your life.

You can speculate on some things. You could even say outright that your spouse or partner is going to need a lot of convincing. You might feel downright certain that since you've got a family to support you can't do what you want. That it would cost you an arm and a leg to go back to school. Or that you're too busy to change careers. Or that no one is going to want to hire a 50-year-old in this field.

But you don't know any of this for sure until you really examine and confront these issues. Until then, they are assumptions. And for the most part, other people, money and time aren't going to be your problem anyway. It's how you *feel* about the issues in your life that will turn them into obstacles.

So let's look at your issues and the concerns (and fears) you have about other people in your life, money and time. Then we'll talk about how to create a plan that lets you confront, handle and manage them. Only then will you be able to work on achieving your goal and know you can still eat, keep a roof over your head and live your life relatively comfortably without too much of a burden.

What are your issues?

These are things like:

- You have two children to support and need to keep your present job.
- You have $5,000 in savings.
- You don't have an education in the field you want to go into.
- Your parents paid for college.
- You are 50 years old.

Write yours here:

_____

_____

_____

_____

_____

_____

_____

_____

_____

_____

_____

_____

_____

_____

_____

_____

_____

What do these have to do with your career change?

Answering that question is actually a liberating step—because you get to vent. You get to bitch and moan and talk about all the "yeah, buts" that are troubling you and will potentially stop you from doing what you say you want. This is the stuff you've wanted to say since page one.

If it helps, start your venting with, "Andrea, don't be ridiculous!"

So for example, you might say: "Andrea, don't be ridiculous! Can't you see that I've got a family to support and I have to think of them first? I can't afford to change careers!"

Or:

"Andrea, don't be ridiculous! Do you think I just sit around and eat bonbons all day? I'm too busy to change careers!"

Or:

"Andrea, don't be ridiculous! Do you think my father is going to support me changing careers after he paid for me to go to college to become a teacher?"

Now let's take a deeper look at the concerns you bring up related to the issues in your life. Let me say first that they are your *opinions* and *assessments* about the realities of your life. Even though you *think* they are the way things are, they are not facts about your life.

The facts are things you *can't* change. Facts are facts. If you're 50, you're 50. If your parents paid for college, they paid for college. If you have two children to support then you have two children to support. But these facts don't determine whether you can make your career change and get what you want. It's how you *feel* about these facts that determines what happens. When your feelings about these facts get in your way, they become head demons. So that's what we work on next.

Based on my work with career changers, head demons seem to fall into five categories. Here are the actual words my clients have used to describe them, and my suggestions on how to confront and manage them.

> Trust because you are willing to accept the risk, not because it is safe or certain.

Head Demon #1:
What if I fail?

*"Going back to school after 30 years is a scary thought.
Will I be able to do it?"*　　　　　—62-year-old health care practitioner

*"I'm not familiar with computers and I don't
have a clue about the Internet."*　　　　　—56-year-old designer

"What if I don't like it?"　　　　　—36-year-old sales representative

*"I have a wife and two kids.
How could I take such a risk?"*　　　　　—41-year-old executive

For the 15 years my client Jackie has been in sales, she has also been in close touch with the restless gnawing in the pit of her stomach. She even knows what to call it—which is more than most people can say. She's dying to be a therapist. She can describe the kinds of problems she wants to help people with and the types of clients she wants to serve. She can picture herself sitting across from a person on a loveseat covered in mauve and seafoam-green flowered fabric with a box of tissues on the coffee table that the client reaches for as he spills his guts about his unhappy relationship. But Jackie is still only *thinking* about this career change, and at this rate, probably always will.

SOME FEAR PARALYZES

*"I am an educator and I have eight years until retirement,
but I am not happy teaching kids. I am
paralyzed with fear at becoming an old woman with no
income if I quit and do what I want to."*

PEGGY, unhappy teacher

"What if it doesn't work?" she wails every time we meet. "What if I can't pay my bills? What if I can't get a job as a therapist? What if I don't like it? What if I waste another four years?"

CONFRONT AND MANAGE IT

OK, what if you don't like it? If you're so miserable now, what's the risk? And just how will you feel if you *don't* try it?

▶ What do you need to do to feel more comfortable? Do you need to know a lot about computers, or is that just something you're worried about? If you do need to know more, learn. Take a course or spend time with a 14-year-old who can show you the ropes. If it's not something that will make or break your success, don't make it an issue.

▶ Do as much research as you can to find out what this new career is really like and if you'd like it. Meet with people who have the kind of job you think you want. Ask hard questions like, "What's your worst day like? What do you dislike about this work? Do you regret being in it? What makes it fulfilling? Why is it worth it? Based on what you know about me and the kind of environment I'm looking for, do you think it's a good fit?"

In Step 7, I referenced the book *Confronting Reality: Doing What Matters to Get Things Right*. The authors, Larry Bossidy and Ram Charan, also talked about one of the most common causes of failures in a business: People don't get information directly from the source; or the information is distorted by people pursuing their own agendas, or by selective hearing, wishful thinking, fear, emotional overinvestment and unrealistic expectations. Their observations also apply to you as an individual in the pursuit of a new career.

One of my clients, who is exploring whether to become a financial planner, is going to great lengths to get information directly from the source. A friend in the business, who lives in another part of the country, offered to put her up at his family's home for a week and allow her to follow him around as he attends meetings and talks to clients. He told her, "I'll teach you whatever I've learned from being in the business 25 years." She plans to take him up on his generous offer. Yes, it's a chunk of time and an investment of money to fly there. But the

SOME WORRY IS NORMAL

"Now that I am facing the schooling to meet my goals, in the back of my mind I sometimes worry, What if I don't make it?"

JOEL, who is studying to be a chiropractor

investment will be valuable in helping her decide if this pursuit is worth putting more time and energy into.

So ask questions, consider the source and dig deeper if you need more data. As you dig, you may find that what it will cost isn't worth it to you.

I had a client who wanted to go from being a project manager in a corporation to a teacher. She was surprised to learn what it would take.

"I would need 30 credit hours in teaching on top of the credit hours for the course work in the subject area I wanted to teach in," she told me. "I did not have enough English, science or math and was looking at 68 credit hours. There were also licensing requirements. There was one program where I could get licensed in just over a year, but the cost was close to $30,000. I'm just not willing to devote that kind of time or money into a career change right now."

It's not that you *can't* do it, but you need to know what you're in for. For example, if you are thinking about becoming a teacher, besides the education, be prepared to go through a "bubble-bursting" time, said Mary Damer, visiting assistant professor at The Ohio State University and a behavior consultant who has observed people who have switched to teaching after being in the military or business. They've had to deal with reality: Today's student is very different from the student of 30 years ago.

"You will need to learn classroom management skills and research-based teaching strategies that have proven successful with at-risk students," she said. This would be helpful to know before you consider such a career.

Whether it's teaching or another career you want to get into, you'll have to overcome hurdles and take steps to succeed. The key is to find out what obstacles you'll face and if you're willing to deal with them. The more you know what you're in for, the easier it will be to stay determined to overcome the difficulties. And that way, the hurdles not only will be expected, but also less significant.

A client who thought about changing careers for more than 20 years finally made peace with his restlessness, did his research and took the leap. He said, "I was so worried I wouldn't like it. But by going forward, at least I'd know it and it would be out of my system instead of my always wondering, 'Should I have done it?'"

HAVE A LITTLE FAITH

Robert Merrill, a baritone with the Metropolitan Opera for 30 years, was an overweight kid from Brooklyn, New York, who stuttered except when he sang. As a teenager, he had a job pushing racks of clothing in Manhattan's garment district, which brought him past the old

HOW WILL I KNOW IF I LIKE IT?

You won't know absolutely, positively, until you actually try it. But you can make an informed choice:

▶ Talk to many people in the field who actually do this work.

▶ Talk to people who don't have an agenda. If, for example, you're exploring an educational program, the school's representative will tell you why it's a great choice. You need to hear other sides as well.

▶ If you're not sure about a particular direction, take it slow. If your career change entails schooling, take one class before enrolling in the entire program. See how you like the field and the school.

▶ Shadow someone who is in the field. Sit in on their meetings, follow them around and see what a typical day is really like.

On October 29, 2004, I asked my client who had waited 36 years to change careers what advice he would give to others. This is a man who did his first career's work well, but whose heart was never in it. He wanted to be a therapist. At this point, he had cancer and had to stop attending classes needed to complete his degree, which he had started working toward just one and a half years earlier.

"If there's something you might enjoy, try it," he said. "Stick your toe into it. Don't say it's too difficult, I can't do it. Don't limit yourself. I was lucky, I had something that interested me. Don't be hesitant and fearful. Sometimes you have to take risks. If you're really unhappy, what do you have to lose?"

It turned out to be a good choice for him. He had found his place. It was a spot where he could share the empathy and compassion he had for others. It changed his life, he told me.

"I got involved in special projects and research projects at the Free Store and Food Bank. I interned at a counseling center. It was wonderful. I felt like I belonged. I was with people I liked and respected and they respected me. It was like a dream come true."

He was quite ill at the time we talked. I sensed that he knew he was offering advice he wished he himself had taken. "There are no guarantees you'll be happy, but life is too short," he said. He died 44 days later.

Metropolitan Opera House, according to his October 2004 obituary in the *New York Times*.

One day he wandered into the Met during a rehearsal of *La Traviata*. He was awestruck and resolved to undertake serious vocal studies—which he did. His first Met audition, in 1941, was a failure. When he auditioned again, in 1944, he made it. The day he died, October 26, 2004, I heard him on a radio interview from years prior talking about his career and how he went from being that kid pushing racks of clothing to an internationally known Verdi baritone. He said, "What did I know—a kid from Brooklyn? But if the desire and the talent is there, it's going to happen."

At some point, every one of my clients who wanted to change careers said, "I'm scared." That's understandable. The issue is managing your fear.

Every choice is an act of faith. There are no guarantees. If you have the desire, you have to be willing to let go of the need to know exactly how it's going to end up.

My client Jackie is focused on having to know how things will turn out. As a result, she wakes up every morning sad and empty. She feels that life is passing her by and finds herself crying a lot—especially every December, as another year ends and a new one approaches.

A more fulfilling approach is to trust that restless gnawing. Explore it without placing demands or conditions on the results. If you've got the talent and the desire is strong enough, as the stuttering kid from Brooklyn said, it's going to happen.

Head Demon #2: What will others think?

"I'm too old to make a career change."   —48-year-old project manager

"They'll think I'm ridiculous."   —60-year-old lawyer

"My father said, 'You'd be giving up everything you worked for.'"   —35-year-old engineer

"My friend said, 'But you don't know anything about advertising.'"   —32-year-old manager

"What will people think of me? That I am nuts to be doing this at my age?"   —54-year-old retail worker

Eighty-six-year-old Joseph DeLeeuw is proof that what others think has nothing to do with what you want and whether it's possible. He's also proof that you are never too old to pay attention to that restless gnawing in the pit of your gut. Born in Winterswijk, Holland, he came to the United States in 1939, as the Nazi invasion was inching closer. Married, with a child to support and new language to learn, he couldn't go to college. Years later, he took night classes and, at 57, got his college degree, graduating magna cum laude. He told his son, Dr. Paul DeLeeuw, "I'd like to go to medical school. Do you think I could go to your old school?"

Despite his son's recommendation, he was not accepted by that or any other American medical school. In so many words, they all told him: You're too old. By the time you finish your residency you'll be 65 and ready to retire. Why should we waste a coveted spot on our roster?

A medical school in the Dominican Republic accepted him. In a town with one paved street, little sanitation and undependable electricity, he studied his all-Spanish texts and lectures by the light of the Coleman lanterns his son brought him.

Despite his age, the obstacles and the naysayers, he never ignored the restless gnawing in the pit of his gut. "Since my early teens I wanted

▶ Who are these other people?

▶ What do you need from them?

▶ Will you lose that if they don't approve of what you're doing?

▶ Are you going to give up what you want because of what they think—or because you're afraid of what they might think?

▶ Why are you letting them run your life?

▶ Why are you asking them what you should do? How would they know?

▶ What do you need to do to endure or cut off the criticism?

to be a doctor," he told me, "to help people who are poor and sick. I'm sentimental and I just wanted to help people."

Joe graduated at 62 and did his residency at Beth Israel Hospital in Manhattan. Working in the emergency room and on call every third night, he was up every morning for 6 A.M. rounds with his 28-year-old fellow residents.

At 66, Joe made his dream come true. In 1983, he opened the Children's Clinic in Dania, Florida. It serves the poor. He works seven days a week, charges $20 a visit, answers his phone any time of the day or night and is as happy as a lark.

Sometimes, well-meaning family members try to influence people. On a *Seinfeld* episode, Jerry Seinfeld, a successful comedian, bounced a check from an old account. His mother, who had just read an article saying that standup comedy is not what it used to be, became worried when she heard about the bounced check. She reminded him about Bloomingdale's executive-training program. He was not fazed by her worry. But the episode reminds me of how other people in your life who care about you may not understand what you're doing and just want to feel that you're safe and secure.

I also had a client who wanted to be involved in the environment. He had told me a wonderful story about how his father had inspired him at a young age to take an interest in the environment by taking him fishing. My client loved the outdoors, conservation, plants and animals, and wanted to be involved in sharing it with others. I later met his father, who was now worried that his son would have difficulty finding a job. Half kidding, he told me, "Maybe I shouldn't have taken him fishing."

CONFRONT AND MANAGE IT

Figure out who those "others" are that you're worried about. Then ask yourself, "Why do I need their approval?"

So let's say your parents did pay for college. If you want to change careers now, what are you worried about? What are you afraid they'll say or do?

This might be the time to finally face a family member or someone you feel holds you back or has certain expectations and to establish new boundaries—even cut ties.

My client, John, a freelance graphic designer, was pursuing a new career direction and had given up all his clients but one—his father's company. His father liked the arrangement, and he really didn't want John to do another type of work.

"I don't think my father believes I can make it on my own," John told me. Although I never talked to his father, based on what John shared, my hunch was that his father might have wanted things to stay

> *"Only care what people think about you*
> *who think reasonable."*
>
> UNKNOWN PHILOSOPHER

ALBERTO HAS A DREAM

Alberto wrote me, after reading one of my columns, "It sure makes me feel better that I'm not the only one that has a dream at 43. I still want to be a singer. I know if I apply myself, I can do it. I've been given a gift to sing, but never really done what it takes to follow through. I have obligations to support my family and so I've always put my dreams on the back burner. I'll be singing at my brother's wedding and I've also performed in musical plays, but now I will be setting my goals higher to achieve one of my long-desired dreams."

status quo. In this arrangement, he could help take care of his son. John wanted to slowly ease out of his work, and had done that, except with his father. He was afraid of what his father would say.

In time, John had a conversation with his father about what he was thinking of doing and how we had worked together. He told him he wanted to cut back on his work with the company to about half of what he was doing at that time and within nine months be totally out of this line of work. He explained the plan to take classes, get a part-time job in his new area of interest and eventually start his own business. It turned out that his father was very supportive and his fears were unwarranted.

SO WHAT IF YOU'RE OVER 40?

Why is that a bad thing? You've got a work ethic every employer is crying out for and crucial experience that can't be duplicated and that younger workers can benefit from. You're a hot commodity!

Why would you reduce everything you are to an age, so that no matter how great your qualifications, your age has become this overwhelming hurdle you can't overcome?

Don't be weakened by your fear that employers think you're washed up. Don't be brought to your knees by the conventional "wisdom" that technology belongs to the young, and that older workers hate change and can't adapt.

Fight back the urge to let stereotypes pervade employers' thinking—and yours. But first you have to recognize how easily you fall into the trap of worrying that no one will want you because they think you can't handle change.

Many older workers are actually fired up about making changes for the better. According to Dr. Tracey Rizzuto, assistant professor of psychology at Louisiana State University, stereotypes about aging employees are simply not true. She said older workers exhibit more willingness to learn new technology than their younger counterparts.

Sure, there are isolated examples of older workers who refuse to budge from old ways—but her study showed that veteran employees:

- See the value of change
- Feel an obligation and loyalty to their coworkers to learn and implement new technology
- Are more inclined to make changes to benefit the organizations
- Are more committed and willing to learn

Another survey, conducted by Harris Interactive, found that 53 percent of older workers are willing to put forth more effort than their younger colleagues.

Of course, some worry is normal. But don't feed the fear. In Step 9, I'll talk more about how to be prepared to deal with an objection if you hear it when marketing yourself.

> *"Fear is created not by the world around us, but in the mind, by what we think is going to happen."*
>
> ELIZABETH GAWAIN

For now, get your head on straight. You don't need a study to tell you how willing you are to change or how much you can contribute. You do, though, need to quell your worry so you can go forward with what you want and later show employers they need not have any misconceptions about you.

She was terrified, but convinced she'd be good enough

"I always dreamed of working in film and am a movie fanatic and dreamed of being on National Public Radio. My first entrée into a regular radio appearance came when I approached the news director of Wyoming Public Radio about being an expert on a talk show he hosts.

"After being a guest, I was scheduled monthly. Then I approached him with the wild and wacky idea of his training me to become a radio producer. He agreed. I received no pay for training, but was paid for segments he aired. Then I got invited to participate in a roundtable discussion for Wyoming Public TV, and a few months later, out of the blue, the program director asked me if I'd like to produce a 12-part documentary TV series. Between my writing experience and natural demeanor on camera, she felt I could be taught the technical skills. If I hadn't volunteered to do the roundtable, she never would have seen me in action.

"I was terrified about producing a TV series. Everything was new to me. I shut down my consulting business to take the job, convinced I'd be good enough so they wouldn't fire me. My love of movies has served me well—especially in choosing camera angles and transitions. I've enjoyed it so much, my husband and I are purchasing digital film equipment and starting our own production company. Switching careers like this was crazy, but I would have been crazier not to have taken the chance to pursue my lifelong dream. Watch out, Emmys and Academy Awards!"

ALIZA SHERMAN RISDAHL, former Internet consultant

Head Demon #3:
I can't afford to do this.

"Money is a realistic concern."   —52-year-old engineer

"I can't afford to quit my job."   —38-year-old salesperson

*"I can't afford to take a lower-paying job
or start back at the first rung."*   —40-year-old lobbyist

When I ask people what exactly it is they can't afford to do, many aren't sure. Some say things like "quit my job" or "go back to school." Others think that because they're changing careers, they will be throwing away all experience and value they had previously, and therefore not be compensated well.

In some careers, you might have to start at the lower end of the pay scale. Other times you can look at how to leverage your past experience and come into a role at a higher level. It all depends. You just don't know yet.

Most people also don't have a clue about their finances, let alone how that affects a career change. When I ask people how much they need to live on or how long they could live without a paycheck, they are rarely able to say. So first figure out what it is you think you can or

> *"I decided to take some time off to regroup,
> think and research what I wanted to do after I was laid
> off. I was afraid because it came at a time where
> we had just remortgaged the house and done
> major remodeling. I was elated and relieved, though,
> to be out of the stress of the position."*
>
> **MARIE**, who went from magazine writer to television producer

can't afford and look at where you stand financially. Then you must assign value to the things in your life.

Answer six key questions to get a handle on where you are and to help you meet your goals, said Rick Krawczeski, vice president of financial planning for McDonald Financial Group in Cincinnati:

1. What are your expenses today? Which ones are fixed? (These are things you have to pay, such as health care, mortgage, rent, car payment and utilities.) Which ones are variables, such as travel, entertainment and going out to eat?

2. What could you do without if you had to?

3. What are you left with? This is how much money you need to live on.

4. What other sources of income, such as a pension, severance pay, rental income or income from a spouse or partner, do you have? How long will these assets last?

5. How much do you have in savings? Can you tap into these assets? What are the tax implications if you do? Given your estimated expenses, how long will your savings last if you need them?

6. What are your long-term goals? If you have children, will you be paying for their college? What about retirement? How will what you're doing now impact those goals? Is that reasonable? Are you willing to modify those goals? Depending on what you say, you may need to reprioritize or give up a goal.

Keep in mind that to answer these questions, you have to know what's most important to you by assigning value to the things in your life.

CONFRONT AND MANAGE IT

- Exactly what is it you can't afford to do?
- What shape are you in financially? What's financially feasible?

When my dentist client met with his financial consultant, they determined that he could go back to school, do occasional project work in the field of dentistry for the two years that it would take to get his degree, be able to pay all his expenses and not disrupt his lifestyle too much. He would need to cut back on some travel plans he had made, but that was a sacrifice he was willing to make.

- What do you need in terms of income to sustain yourself?
- Can you afford to take time off and explore a new position or go back to school full-time?
- Do you need to work part-time? If so, how much money do you need to make?
- Can you live off another source of income, and if so, for how long?
- What's your time line for making your career change?
- Do you need to go back to school? Will you need a few courses or a degree? What will it cost?
- Even if you have to cut back financially, is it worth it to have peace of mind and time to regroup?

Don't act like most people do and immediately conclude you "can't afford it" without first doing a reality check on finances.

Head Demon #4: I should hold on to what I've got.

"I was steeped in old messages that I could hear from my mother. I should be a doctor. It's a good job. Why would you give that up?"
—45-year-old doctor

Only two out of thousands of people have ever told me they love change, and I don't believe even those two. They may love to go into a company and change processes or improve the way the firm does business, get rid of deadwood or turn around a bad situation. But when it comes to themselves, people don't love change. Change dismantles your life. It upsets the apple cart—even the smallest things.

Besides all the work that change brings on, most of us would rather stick with what we are familiar with. When the New York subway was celebrating its 100th year of service in October 2004, I heard one of its workers—who works all night in that dark, damp and dingy place—

say in a radio interview that he's more comfortable walking the tracks than the streets of New York. Why in the world would he say that?

"Because I know the environment. I know the pitfalls," he explained.

That's how we humans operate. We like to know what's around the corner. We think we have more control that way.

Another reason we stick with what we have—even when it's not what we want—is because it's hard to part with what has defined so much of who we are. My dentist client stayed in his career for 36 years. He got into dentistry for several reasons—one being because "It was prestigious, and it was a big deal to make money."

"My family didn't have any money when I was growing up. Now I was successful and making money and I liked being able to buy things for my family and take vacations."

Writer Tom Wolfe has a theory about this too. "It all has to do with status," he said in a 2004 article in the *New York Times Magazine*. "Social behavior is almost always determined by status conscious-ness—an instinct to preserve your place in the social pecking order." Status details, as Wolfe calls them, include "where a person thinks he belongs and, more important, where he wants to stay. In the Wolfean scheme, people aren't so much interested in scaling the social ladder as in clinging to their own, hard-earned rung."

By clinging to his own hard-earned rung, my client had created a life of despair and anxiety. He was constantly torn between maintaining his status and following his heart. The closer we got to defining new career directions for him to explore, the more anxious he became

> *"One hundred percent of the people around there agree we need to change, but 90 percent of them don't really want to change themselves."*
>
> **NOBUYUKI IDEI,**
> CEO, Sony Corporation, *Fortune*, April 2005

and the tighter he held on to his old life, saying over and over in our meetings, "I don't know what to do, I just don't know what to do."

CONFRONT AND MANAGE IT

- What are you holding on to?
- What do you gain from it?
- What is it keeping you from getting or doing?
- What will you lose if you give it up?
- Is it worth more than the new career satisfaction you want?

Sometimes people don't want to part with something because they think it's the only way someone values them. Or it's what they value so much about themselves. My client John, the graphic designer whose main client was now his father's company, wanted desperately to stop doing work that he found lonely and meaningless. "There's a part of me that doesn't want to let go of it," he told me after we had worked together awhile and he was absolutely certain about his new career path.

"I now have a vision of my future, a path of how to get there, the confidence in my ability to make it happen and the courage to act on what needs to be done. I'm not turning back now. It's the right thing to do."

But he was still working for his father—even thinking of extending his "cut-the-cord" date, saying, "The work is a distraction now. The more I work, the more unhappy I am. But I'm sustaining this facade that I have a job and I make money. I have guilt about not earning money. And there is some value in doing work I do well. Without this, what will I have?"

> *"I begged for jobs as a production assistant,*
> *but they were hard jobs to get. I drove a cab, was a*
> *Xerox messenger and my wife helped support me.*
> *It was temporary employment*
> *here and there, unemployment here and there."*
>
> OLIVER STONE, film director

After talking through these issues, John speculated that he was afraid to give up what he hated because he believed his father wouldn't value him as a person anymore. In addition, he didn't want to give up the value *he* saw himself having by doing a job well—even if he hated it.

Finally, he decided, "I'd be more responsible to myself, my family and the universe if I stopped polluting it with my bad energy and stress and get out of that work. And, I'd have a more authentic relationship with my father."

After we evaluated the loss of income he'd experience from quitting this work and what else he'd gain, he concluded, "There's no question about it—nothing in my life will suffer if I quit doing this work. Only my pride."

Whatever your reason for clinging to what you have—even if it is a dark and dingy place—you know what to expect. But is that what you want more of?

Head Demon #5:
It's not a good time to change careers.

"I don't have time."   —Everyone says this

"The time commitment of two years to study and do an internship would be huge. I just got married, and it would cut into our social lives and our relationship."
                                                                 —60-year-old man

"With the economy the way it is, changing careers could be risky."
                                        —40-year-old information technology worker

Is there ever a good time to change your life? It's never going to be convenient, I can tell you that. And if you're waiting until you have no obligations, the economy is right, or the moon and stars are aligned perfectly with Jupiter and Mars, well, you may as well forget it ever happening.

Yes, you will need to work out the details that affect your daily life and those who are close to you. Yes, it needs to be enough of a priority for you to tamper with your life. And yes, you will have to sacrifice something—time, money, sleep, vacations—whatever. But if you're wise enough to notice that restless gnawing in the pit of your gut, be wise enough to make the time to act on it.

CONFRONT AND MANAGE IT

If you are worried about the time that this process will require, first figure out how you spend your time to get a realistic picture of where it goes and how much you can and want to devote to your career change.

- Look at each day of the week. How many hours do you work on average each week? Besides sleep, how do you spend the rest of your time? What about weekends?
- What can you cut out that's not serving you well, so you can focus more on this career change?
- What is it going to take to make this change? Will you need to go back to school? For how long? Approximately how many hours of your time will that take? What exactly will you be making time to do? How much time does that require?
- Do you have flexibility during the day in which you can work on your career change?
- Can you take classes through your employer? Can you take one or two vacation days a month to devote to your career change?

If you are concerned that circumstances just aren't right for a career change, figure out:

- The perfect circumstances in which to change
- When those circumstances will come about
- What you need to do to make those circumstances possible
- If those circumstances will ever be possible

"Ask yourself, what would I do if I weren't afraid? Then do whatever that is."

SPENCER JOHNSON,
author of Yes or No, The Guide to Better Decisions

If it's highly unlikely that circumstances will ever be perfect, what are you waiting for?

MY "SO WHAT?" TEST

When one of my clients brings up a concern, I apply my "So what?" test. While this exercise has been known at first to generate some annoyance on their part, it always helps us work through an issue. Here's how it might go.

ROB: I want to change careers, but I have two children to support and I need to keep my present job.

ME: *So what*? How does that affect your desire to change careers?

ROB: Well, I can't quit my job.

ME: Who said anything about quitting your job?

ROB: Well then how do I figure out what I want and then look for a new job?

ME: What, besides work, do you fit in your life now?

ROB: Time with my kids. Golf and tennis.

ME: How do you manage that? How do you find the time?

ROB: I put the golf and tennis dates on my calendar. My kids have activities that are scheduled and I plan to attend.

ME: That's how you'll do this career-change thing. You'll put dates on your calendar to do these exercises and to conduct research, hold informational meetings, create a new resume, inquire about positions, or take classes if you need to.

ROB: But there's not enough time to do all that.

ME: How much time do you think 'all that' will take?

ROB: I don't know.

ME: First, you need to decide how much time you *want* it to take in your life and create a time line for meeting your objective. Then, let's look at two things. One, how you spend your time now. Two, what you might cut out of your life that's not serving you well so you can focus on spending that chunk of time on your career change.

So, first, how much time do you want to devote to your career change and when do you want to be job hunting for a new career position?

ROB: At this point, five hours a week. And I guess I want to complete this in one year.

Then we stroll through his life together and break his down time into weeks and then into days, and look at how he spends those hours. We usually find between 6 and 15 hours of television that can be cut. (The U.S. government study, the American Time Use Survey, found that people tend to spend roughly half their free time watching TV.) We also round up several hours on the weekend that can be used differently.

Since Rob decides that, for now, he wants to spend two and half hours on Sunday afternoon and two and half hours on Thursday evening on his career change, we talk about the activities he'd focus on.

This does take discipline and planning. But Rob said he wanted this badly enough and was willing to incorporate the new activities into his life by cutting out some things and shifting around others.

My client Lisa, who has two young children, found it difficult to establish a routine. "It's hard to follow a routine with young kids—at least it was for me. I needed to network in the evenings and weekends, so I attended some women's educational and leadership events—which is where I found the lead that led to my job."

You have to be realistic. As with anything, don't commit to doing things you're not willing to follow through on. When I made the decision to start an exercise program, I knew I was only willing to put 20 minutes a day into it and I told that to the trainer I was working with. I know I could do more, but 20 minutes fit my life and I committed to do it without great sacrifice. I just got up a half hour earlier each day and I got results.

The same goes for this process. Decide how much time you're willing to invest. The more you do and the faster you do it, the bigger and quicker the results. So, if you want a career that requires a new degree, you have to decide what your time line is and if you will go back to school full- or part-time. A part-time commitment will obviously take you longer.

BITTERSWEET REALITY

Everything has a price. And the price to pay for what you want can get in your way—if you don't pick apart your fears about that and figure out a way around or through them.

Aside from a way to confront and manage these issues, your desire for what you want must be stronger than what you're afraid of.

How to find time to do this
career change

Let's say you work, on average, nine hours a day. The average commute to and from work is 26 minutes. You sleep seven hours a day (although Americans sleep an average 8.6 hours, according to that U.S. government study, American Time Use Survey). That leaves you with 7.5 hours a day to eat, be with your family, play the piano, do housework, do Pilates, read, analyze the stock market, watch TV, be with friends or put time into your career change. That's 37.5 hours of time that you have Monday through Friday. You get to choose how you want to spend it.

You also have weekends. Depending on your life, your "free" time could range from as many as 35 hours to a few hours that you have to put into your career change.

One man I knew, who had been an advertising copywriter for 12 years, was working on becoming a screenwriter and selling his scripts and eventually directing movies. After an eight-hour day at the advertising agency he worked for, he'd come home, have dinner and watch a little television. From about 10 P.M. until 2 or 3 A.M. every day, he focused on his screenwriting and movie projects.

So, how much of that time are you willing to devote to your career change? And how are you going to fit that into your day?

You need to know in your heart of hearts that you want a change badly enough to quiet your fears and go forward anyway.

You may have to go back to school to qualify for your next career, and while you're at it, make less money than you're used to. You may get rejected fifty times before someone says, "Yes, we'll hire you." But I can promise that it will be impossible to find something better if you don't first want it badly and believe you can have it.

IF SOMETHING IS GETTING IN YOUR WAY

1. What worries you about making this career change?

2. Why is that a problem?

3. If it were resolved, what would the situation be like?

4. What do you need to do to make that happen?

5. What's stopping you from doing that?

6. What do you need to change to fix that? What do you need to ask someone else?

7. What do you need to change inside yourself?

8. Now what are you going to do?

No one can guarantee how successful you will be. But I can guarantee that you will never be victorious in finding more satisfaction if you don't have the courage to act despite your fear.

Actor Christopher Reeve, who became paralyzed in 1995 and died in 2004, once said, "I get pretty impatient with people who are able-bodied, but are paralyzed for other reasons."

Someone else said it a little more crudely, but effectively nevertheless. On an episode of the HBO program *Six Feet Under*, the character David, who sees and has conversations with his dead father, is thinking about his life. His father tells him, "You can do anything, you lucky bastard. You're alive."

Heed their words and get impatient with yourself for this reason: You want more out of your life and have the ability to go after it.

IF YOU START TO FREAK OUT

At any point in this process, you might get nervous. Even if you think you have worked out all the kinks, like John—who after eight months of working toward his new career direction was afraid to let go of the work he hated—things crop up. Don't freak out and give up.

Instead, first notice what's getting in your way. Are you worried about whether it will work out? Are you concerned about what others will think? Do you think you can't afford it? Are you worried about letting go of something? Do you think you don't have time?

Then go forward anyway:

- Let go of your need to know exactly how it's going to turn out.
- Choose to live in accordance with who you are—not what others want you to be.
- Assign value to what matters to you so can afford to go after what you want.
- Let go of what you're clinging to that is holding you back.
- Make the time to act on what you say you want.

MAP OUT HOW YOU'LL ACHIEVE YOUR OBJECTIVE—BASED ON YOUR REALITY

Remember my client who wanted to help people make healthier lifestyle choices by assessing and advising them on nutrition, diet and exercise? At this point in the process, he was really pumped. He could see himself doing this, and he was ready to go forward to meet his goal by a certain date.

But then there were those realistic issues in his life, and of course his concerns and fears about them. He began to wonder—just like you will—is this practical? Can I really do this? The answer is almost always yes, but not without adjusting some things. So we walked through the issues he needed to confront to map out a plan for him to meet his goal.

WHAT NEARLY EVERY CAREER
CHANGER TELLS ME

"I wish I had done it sooner."

Confront your issues and develop a plan to resolve them.

For example, he needed to develop a strategy for winding down his full-time job so he'd have 25 hours a week to put into his career change while still making a certain amount of money. We talked about whether to wind it down or possibly get out of it completely and look into getting a job in a health club, hospital or facility where he could gain experience working with clients on health care issues. So he first needed to create a short-term plan to meet his long-term objective. In other words, working in another job while working on his next career.

To explore the part-time job option, we created a list of organizations that fit his criteria. Then we looked at his other concerns.

One concern was that he wouldn't be taken seriously because he didn't have any "real" experience. He had successfully advised friends on developing good eating habits, exercise and healthier lifestyles. But he didn't feel he had the credentials or solid knowledge to do this work in another environment.

"What do you need to be ready?" I asked him.

"I need to round out my confidence," he said.

"What will that take?" I asked.

"For one thing, I need to get certified as a personal trainer and find out which programs I can do in one year. I want more knowledge on obesity, nutrition and disease."

IT HELPS TO BE AN IDEALISTIC REALIST

Realize two things:

1. **There is no easy path.**
2. **When you choose one thing, you sacrifice something else.**

Then think through the steps you'll need to take to get what you want. Ask yourself: Am I willing to do that?

> *"I was very scared and I had to face my fears.*
> *Would I be good enough? If you are making a change,*
> *have patience, ask questions, follow your heart,*
> *face your fears, surround yourself with people*
> *who have your best interests at heart, and most of all,*
> *don't be afraid to ask for help."*
>
> CHARLIE, who became a teacher at age 50

Break whatever "it" is into doable tasks—one step at a time.
So we came up with a list of five things he needed to do first:

1. Research personal-trainer programs that can be completed in one year.
2. Find out when the next courses in nutrition, anatomy and physiology were being offered at his local universities and what it would take to get enrolled.
3. Research local professional groups that support like-minded professionals so he could learn more about options, training and the kinds of positions he might like.
4. Find books and information on obesity.
5. Think more about what areas of knowledge he felt inept in besides the ones he had already identified.

He also felt he needed to fine-tune his own eating and exercise habits so he was living the kind of life he wanted to help others create. To do this and incorporate his other five activities, we developed a plan of how he would spend his day, Monday through Friday: Five hours in his part-time job, two hours working out at the gym, two to four hours on research and job search.

Work that plan.
As he worked the plan, activities changed. He began attending classes and studying instead of doing research. He became more focused on

what kinds of classes he wanted to take. After six months of working his plan, he had a new list with a new time line. He now decided he wanted to start his own business. So, aside from the new certification and continuing education he felt he needed, he created a "to do" list of things it would take to start his business, including:

- A concise definition of his target market and how he'd reach them
- An economic model of how his company would make money
- A discussion with his wife about how this would affect their finances
- An overall business plan

He had his ups and downs (which I'll tell you about in a later chapter when I talk about how to stay focused and committed in this process), but after one year, he told me, "I can see this career now. I know I can make it happen and I have the confidence to act on it. I could start it tomorrow."

Remember Will, the contractor who had great instincts, persuasive writing skills and a knack for assimilating complex information and com-

"It's not going to work if you don't believe in it. Just believe."

Actor JOHNNY DEPP, as J. M. Barrie in the movie *Finding Neverland*

municating it in two minutes or less in a powerful way? Although he had some experience in applying those skills, he realized he needed to hone his writing skills to be able to contribute them to the business world.

He didn't say, "Woe is me, I'll never be able to work in business since I've never done it, I'm over 30 and who's going to want to hire me?" He figured out the things he needed to do to achieve his goal and make himself marketable to corporate America.

He went back to evening college and took marketing communications classes. He got more experience by developing the strategy and ads for a local political campaign—getting his first paid consulting role in public relations and advertising. In that process, he met the owner of an advertising agency, which eventually led to his first full-time job in advertising. He didn't have to get a degree. Building on his experience, he was able to demonstrate that, along with his skills, determination and self-initiative, he had the potential to be a valuable resource for a company.

How to work your plan

1. Write your new career objective here:

_____

_____

_____

_____

_____

_____

_____

_____

_____

_____

_____

_____

Dumb moves:
Going to school to buy time

Dozens of people tell me they're going back to school to get a master's degree or another undergraduate degree because they think it will make it easier to get a job in a new field. When I asked them what field or how they think it will make them more valuable, they don't know. They have just heard that it's a good thing to do. Besides, they tell me, "I don't know what else to do."

Sometimes I meet them *after* they have gotten their degree and they are in the same boat they were in before they spent two years and thousands of dollars on more schooling.

It doesn't help when you read comments like this one posted in an article at CFO.com. A former teacher who went to business school said, "You don't even have to know what you want to do when you enroll." As he put it, after graduation, he fell into his next career as a bank-lending executive by accident and now likes what he does.

I'm happy for him. It can happen. But that's not what most people tell me happens to them. I'm all for continuing education—if it supports your future and it's a sensible return on investment.

2. What issues could get in your way of making that happen?

_____

_____

_____

_____

_____

_____

3. What do you need to do to confront them?

_____

_____

_____

_____

_____

_____

4. What do you need to do to overcome or resolve them?

_____

_____

_____

_____

_____

_____

5. What specific steps do you need to take?

_____

_____

_____

_____

_____

_____

_____

6. Do you need a short-term plan to help you get to your long-term objective? If so, what is it? Is there a short-term job that you can take related to your next career that will make you more valuable? If so, what are those possible options?

_____

_____

_____

_____

_____

_____

_____

_____

_____

_____

_____

_____

_____

_____

_____

_____

_____

_____

_____

_____

_____

_____

Step 9

Target them, find them, get and keep their attention.

L et's fast-forward here, assuming you have completed any necessary education and worked out the kinks to move your plan forward and meet your objective. Or that you're near the point when you will be ready to complete your plan. Either way, we'll focus on the next phase: finding your new career position.

In this step, we'll spend a lot of time on how you'll speak about yourself to prospective employers and others who can assist you in your job search. But first, we'll discuss how to sniff out opportunities and the right people to market yourself *to*. Because you need a strategy.

Specifically, you'll figure out four things:

1. Who's your target?
2. Where do you find them?
3. How do you get their attention?
4. How do you keep their attention?

Who's your target?

Even though you're raring to go, don't talk to just anyone. That would *not* be strategic. If you talk to every Tom, Dick and Harry, you potentially spend valuable time in nonproductive, low-return-on-investment activities. Let's make the most of your valuable time and discuss what to do with whom and why, in order to discover your next career position.

IF YOU'RE STILL FUZZY OR NEARLY CLUELESS

What to do and who to target

Even if you don't know exactly what your next career is called, by now you have some sense of the industry (or types of industries) you see yourself joining. Write them down. What related or ancillary industries work hand in hand with your target industry? Write them down too.

For example, if you're interested in health care, your related industries or companies could include pharmaceutical, long-term health care facilities, ambulatory health care services, manufacturers of medical devices and instruments, hospitals, health professional associations, medical practices, health insurance companies, rehabilitation and physical therapy or home health care services.

Looking at your lists, develop a line-up of *companies* that fit within those industries. If you're focused on a specific geographical area, which are the companies and organizations located there? You can find them in various places: the chamber of commerce in that area, through articles in the local business and metropolitan newspapers, in directories that list companies in that particular industry, by talking to people and through online searches. Some online sources for company information are Brint.com, Hoovers.com, Wetfeet.com, Vault.com, LibrarySpot.com and Bizweb.com. To view annual reports, go to annualReports.com, reportgallery.com or prars.com.

From there, you can target *people* in those industries and companies. Dig up their names from directories, an online search, through news releases written about the company, through information on the company's Web site or by asking other people. If all else fails, call up the company, find a live human being and ask, "Can you tell me who is the manager in charge of information technology?" (or whatever area you're focusing on).

You can also find companies by buying lists. For example, if you go to ZapData.com, you can buy lists that will name companies by location, industry and size.

So to recap, here's your basic strategy:

1. Start broad, by looking at *industries.*
2. Narrow your target by listing *companies* in those industries.
3. Then focus on *people* in those companies or other organizations who can offer you help.

The main reason you're targeting these people:

To meet (minimally, talk by telephone) and get information.

You want to introduce yourself, tell them about your new career objective and ask for their advice on how someone with your background and interest might fit into the industry.

Why? Because you're fuzzy or nearly clueless, and what they know can help you get clearer. They know:

- Trends in the industry
- Problems and needs of the industry and in specific companies
- Other people in the industry
- Obstacles you might run into
- What qualifications you need
- Who's leaving a job or about to be asked to leave
- Positions that might be created in specific companies (theirs included) in response to a need
- New businesses coming to town
- Ways to contact decision makers

You can ask them about the best way to find a job in this industry or a specific company. In that conversation, they may tell you about openings they've heard about or be willing to refer you to someone they know in your targeted industry.

People who work in a health care facility, for instance, know what's happening in a related business or industry because they deal with people there. They know people who sell medical instruments or who oversee health-related professional organizations. They know colleagues through professional associations.

But since you're fuzzy, your main goal is to get more information that will help you *learn about the needs* of your industry and *what kinds of jobs exist that meet your career objective.* Since you also want to *discover positions* (once you're clearer), your other goal is to make a good impression. Then folks will be more inclined to offer you names of people in the industry or companies where they suggest you look. If they don't like you, they won't refer you to their associates. Later in this step, we'll talk about how to make a good impression.

IF YOU'RE CLEARER OR CRYSTAL CLEAR

What to do and who to target

You'll do the same thing a fuzzy or clueless career changer would: create a list of the type of *industry* or *industries* you see yourself fitting into, and from that develop a roster of *companies* that fit that industry. From there, you can directly target the *people* in the companies you think you might want to work for.

Two main reasons you're targeting these people:

1. To meet and get information
2. To explore working for their company

On the getting-information front, you want to introduce yourself and talk to people within companies in your industry, in order to tell them about your new career objective and ask for their advice on how best to find a job in this industry. In that conversation, they may tell you about openings they've heard about or be willing to refer you to someone they know in other companies.

Why would you do this, even though you know exactly what you want? Because you don't know everything there is to know, and they can tell you more about:

- Trends in the industry
- Problems and needs of the industry and in specific companies—including theirs
- Other people in the industry and in specific companies
- Obstacles you might run into
- What qualifications you need
- Who's leaving a job or about to be asked to leave
- Positions that might be created in specific companies (theirs included) in response to a need
- New businesses coming to town
- Ways to contact decision makers

On the second front—exploring working for their company—you'll want to introduce yourself and explain your new career objective and how you would like to contribute to the company. You're meeting to tell company decision makers that you want to enter this field and why, what you bring to the table and that you want to offer all of that to *them*.

Part of your goal is to get information—which is what you *can* solely focus on. But since you're clearer, and assuming you like what you know about the company, you also can focus on discovering positions and needs in companies and directly applying for jobs.

One word of caution: Do not set up a networking meeting (telling the person the objective of the meeting is to get their advice) and then ask the person if they have a job for you at their company. That is misleading.

Yes, it could be that in a networking meeting the person discovers how much they like you, see value in you and want to talk about you working for their company. But you get to that point because *they* bring up the fact that they have a position. You don't ask.

Whether you're meeting to get information or apply for a job, one or more of three things will hopefully happen:

1. You will inspire people to refer you to others in companies where you want to work.
2. People will tell you about open positions they've heard about in the industry.
3. People will consider you as a prospect for their company now or in the future.

HOW BETH FOUND HER TARGETS, AND WHAT HAPPENED NEXT

To illustrate how to identify the companies and people you want to target, and how the process can work, let's use my client Beth, the engineer.

Beth designed airplane engines, analyzed and researched data and engine performance, created engine models and evaluated product capabilities. She communicated with management and customers to determine their needs and participated on teams that evaluated product design.

She enjoyed using these skills—but not with airplane engines and in the engine manufacturer environment.

"It's not that engines aren't important—and of course it's vital that they be made right," she told me, almost apologetically, "but I just don't care about them."

Instead, she wanted to analyze and research products and technology that intrigued her and were aesthetically designed.

She wanted to communicate with customers—but not ones who made airplane engines. She liked the thought of working with customers who, as she put it, "use and care about everyday, functional products that look cool."

She also wanted to build on her curiosity and interest in digital technology and customizable products and the other things she cared about: color, aesthetics and ergonomics.

Beth lit up when she talked about stylishly designed coffeemakers and washing machines, car instruments that you can change the color of on the fly, color-changing globes you can program to respond to Internet data, flat-panel televisions, heating and cooling drawers, programmable thermostats, robot vacuum cleaners and mowers, and watches with unconventional functionality. She wanted to be involved with such products.

In her earlier research, she had met with engineers, architects, designers and sales people in industrial-design firms, college professors and people who worked for manufacturers. From those discussions, she concluded that she didn't want to be a product designer. Instead, she sought a role where she could track emerging technology and help deliver it to others in the form of cool, everyday products.

Here's how she described her objective: "I want to explore a liaison role between the designer and the people who want to buy aesthetically pleasing, stylish, useful products that they use every day."

Now she was ready to dig deeper to figure out if there are such roles within companies, and if so, which companies. Then she would, hopefully, discover which of these companies had openings or might create such positions.

So, as a starting point, it made sense for her to target companies that make the kinds of products she liked. She also targeted companies that might want to expand into making these kinds of products. She developed a list of innovative manufacturers within a 500-mile radius of where she lived by reading industrial-design publications and Web sites that discussed product development. She asked people in her new network to suggest company names. She looked for potential ways to put herself in front of as many people in the industrial-design industry as possible. She registered for a national conference of professionals in product design, bought a plane ticket to Philadelphia and attended the conference for two days.

Before she left, we discussed objectives she wanted to achieve, who she wanted to talk to, how best to approach them and questions she wanted to ask. We also practiced how she'd talk about herself (I'll get to that in a moment). She had her resume with her to hand out at appropriate times. And she created and gave out a well-designed business card that on the back had her "Objective" and bulleted points under the heading "Proven Abilities."

Besides walking the aisles of company trade show booths, she told me, "I 'worked the room' in between seminars." This was quite a feat for her, because she is a quiet, reserved person who likes to observe.

"One person led me to another," she said. "We spent time talking and brainstorming about my place in the industry. I got some really great ideas."

But it wasn't until she heard a vice president of product development for a manufacturer speak in a seminar that her role came into focus and she went from clear to crystal clear.

"He showed their products that either have or will utilize technology to solve problems and customer issues. I became so excited! I saw how my experience in thermofluid sciences could be of value to a company. I knew I had to talk to this man, who had a similar background as mine. After his seminar, I waited my turn in line to talk to him. It's kind of a blur, but I gave him my background in about 20 seconds and told him how fascinated I was with the innovative ways he was incorporating technology into his products. I asked him who he relied upon to provide technology.

"He said, 'Right now, I rely upon myself.' Then he said that he had a position open, a technology watchdog-type function. A person who would work for him to keep track of emerging technologies and determine how they could be applied to their products. It sounded like a dream job!"

So Beth not only got ideas on where she fit into the industry, she stumbled upon an actual job opening. It can happen.

By the way, the company flew her to town for an interview within the week. She didn't get the job; but meeting this man, interviewing for the position and seeing what one company called this role helped her form a well-defined picture of her ideal new career. She would not have gotten that far if she hadn't first understood and then been able to describe to others her strengths and what she knew and cared about. Her understanding of herself—and then being able to articulate this to others—helped them see a place for her, doing what she had imagined.

1. Through newspaper or online postings or hearing about an opening from a recruiter

2. Stumbling upon it through strategic, purposeful conversations with people you've targeted

3. Discovering that someone you targeted through your strategic conversations or were referred to has a need for you and wants to create a job to meet this need

The most high-return-on-investment activities above are numbers 2 and 3.

Spend most of your time talking to people. Yes, incorporate number 1 into your overall job search strategy. But plopping yourself in front of your computer and sending your resume to job sites all day is not a strategy. It's one activity that's part of an overall strategy.

Beth continued to research and talk to more people in companies that fit her ideal profile. The experience and exposure to so many people strengthened her confidence and helped her see, "My skills are transferable. There's a place for me."

Rouse the troops:
How to get someone's attention

Basically, there are two activities in which you're trying to get others to participate:

1. Information gathering (you could call this networking)
2. Discussing jobs at their company

To entice them to participate in either activity, you have to *get* and
hold their attention long enough so they'll say, "Yes, let's meet."

You try to gain their attention by calling them up, writing a letter, sending e-mail or making the most of an unexpected moment.
Whether you are successful in getting them to agree to meet with you
will depend on how effective you are in what you say to them in this
initial communication.

In all modes of communication, the key is to take one relationship at a time. Even if you have 25 people you want to target, don't
send out form letters or e-mails. That doesn't mean you must reinvent
the wheel with each note. But each note or phone call is customized to
that person. Here's how you do it.

First, create a template of the points to always cover *when asking
someone to give you advice:*

1. Why you want to talk to *them* specifically, including
   how you found them
2. What your situation is
3. What you want from them
4. How you'll follow up

Sample letter or e-mail asking someone to meet with you and give you advice:

Dear Ms. Lingo:

Your comments in the April issue of *Meeting Planner Pro* about tracking your value to companies by benchmarking corporate rates vs. negotiated rates were excellent. As I am new to the field, you energized me to be more innovative.

Having just completed my training to become a Certified Meeting Professional, I am exploring where I'd fit into the industry. I have planned and organized more than 20 successful special events for several professional associations as a volunteer while working full-time as an attorney. At the end of this year, I will leave the legal profession to pursue my passion to become a meeting planner.

Since we are both located in the Cleveland area, I am writing to ask if you would be willing to meet to give me more insight into the meeting-planning field. I know your time is valuable. Would you be open to holding a brief meeting within the next few weeks?

I will follow up with you by phone early next week.

Thank you.

Sincerely,
Phillip Holinski

In a phone call, you could cover these four points by saying:

Hello, Ms. Lingo, my name is Phillip Holinski. I read your comments in the April issue of Meeting Planner Pro. *And as someone who's new to meeting planning, I found them really inspiring. I just completed my training to become a Certified Meeting Professional and am exploring where I'd fit in. I have planned and organized more than 20 special events for several professional associations as a volunteer while working full-time as an attorney. At the end of this year, I will leave the legal profession to pursue my passion to become a meeting planner.*

Since we are both located in Cleveland, I am calling to see if you would be willing to meet to give me more insight into this field. I know your time is valuable. Would you be open to holding a brief meeting in the next few weeks?

What gets their attention? For starters, your opening, which is customized to the person you're approaching. You base this on something you have read—about them or their company—or on comments they made in an interview or during a previous interaction you may have had with them.

Just think of how you'd feel if you got a letter from a person pointing out something you once said in a presentation or in an article and how much impact your words had on them. You'd probably be a little surprised, maybe flattered. So the writer of this note not only got your attention, but when they go on to ask you for your advice, you'd be more open to offering it or referring them to someone else.

Or perhaps the writer has taken the time to find out about your company's long-term goals and brings those up in the opening. You'd be more inclined to want to help that person than someone who writes, "I am looking for a job in the meeting-planning industry and wondered if you would give me the benefit of your years of knowledge by holding a networking meeting."

For the most part, the rest of the information in your communication can be similar, but may need tweaking. By always covering these four points, you get the person to read further, because you quickly get to the crux of what you want and what will happen next. They'll be expecting— perhaps even looking forward to—your follow-up phone call.

Next, create a template of the points to always cover *when asking someone to meet to discuss possible employment at their company:*

1. Why you're interested in *them* and *their* company in particular
2. What your situation is and why it would make sense to talk
3. Overview of your qualifications
4. How you'll follow up

Sample letter asking someone to meet to explore employment at their company:

Dear Ms. Lingo:

When I read about your vision to expand your meeting-planning services to the association market, it seemed as if there might be a match between your needs and my expertise.

Although technically new to the profession, I am no stranger to the field. I have planned and organized over 20 successful special events for several professional associations while fulfilling my responsibilities as an attorney, and have recently completed training as a Certified Meeting Professional. I will be leaving the legal profession this year to pursue my passion to become a meeting planner.

My qualifications include:

- More than 10 years of planning and coordinating successful conventions and special events for up to 400 attendees
- Expertise in negotiations and contracts
- The ability to envision the big picture as well as details
- A reputation for always delivering a memorable experience

Since your goals include expanding into the association market, I thought it might make sense to meet. I will call your office next week to explore your interest.

Thank you.

Sincerely,
Phillip Holinski

TALKING TO STRANGERS, AND OTHER CREATIVE APPROACHES

Sometimes you will have the chance to connect with someone on the fly because a situation simply presents itself. Take for example this interaction that took place on a street in Los Angeles.

Jason was trying to get into the movie-production industry—specifically as an assistant director. He had some experience as an assistant director on several short movies. One night he was standing outside a theater passing out fliers to promote one of these short films, when he saw a well-known movie director whom he respected and would have loved to work for. The director was getting into his car with his wife as Jason approached him and said hello. He told the director, "I owe you ten dollars."

The director asked him why. Jason said, "I always told myself if I ran into you I'd give you ten dollars, because five years ago I sneaked into one of your films and another director's film. So I owe you ten dollars."

The director asked him what the other film was and when Jason told him, said, "That was a good film, but you don't owe me ten dollars."

"I insist," said Jason. So, the director took the money and Jason said he'd like him to have his business card as well. The card described him as an assistant director. He said, "Even though I'm an assistant director, if I could get on to one of your films, I'd work as a production assistant."

The director thanked Jason for his card and the ten dollars and said, "You're on the top of the list."

Whether you're contacting someone cold or someone you've been referred to, or you happen upon a person, treat each one with individual care. Do what you say you're going to do, thank people, follow up and keep in touch. The key to discovering your new career position will largely be based on how well you treat one relationship at a time.

Keep their attention once you get it

Once someone has agreed to talk, make it worth their time. Deliver what you promised, which is either:

1. A conversation that provokes questions and helpful input, which in turn makes them feel useful and good about helping you or telling someone else about you
2. An exploration between their needs and your qualifications

Everything you've done up to now has prepared you for this. In a way, you're different from when we first started this process. From the standpoint of how you see yourself, you're no longer a sales and marketing person, a technical writer, an engineer, an information techie, a doctor or whatever your last or present career is.

You're someone with extensive *knowledge* in a particular area. You have *experience*, *education* and transferable *strengths*. And you are clear that you want to build on all of that while incorporating your interest in this new direction you've chosen.

So now you can see yourself as a walking, talking body of skills, knowledge, experience and passion. You're not a title. You're a valuable commodity ready to put all of that, including your new education (if you have one) or knowledge (if you've learned new things), toward your next career position.

That's how you're going to present yourself to the world—potential employers and people you'll be targeting to hold networking meetings: as a walking, talking body of valuable skills, useful knowledge, beneficial experience and passion.

SAY IT WITH AMAZING GRACE

When you talk about yourself, you won't necessarily bring up everything or gab in great detail about some things from your past. They may not be relevant. Certain experiences or knowledge may not support your new objective. But you're not going to throw *away* your experience either. How much of it you'll mention and exactly what you bring up will depend on how *relevant* it is to what you want to do next. Relevant—that's a word you'll hear me use a lot. It's the key to marketing yourself in your new career. Too much information overwhelms people. Relevant information helps you influence people in how you want them to see you.

You have already done some talking to people, in Step 7, while researching your next career. What you prepared and delivered back then will come in handy now.

Remember, in that step, how my client Beth set up the conversation to get someone's advice? She used a 30-second introduction that included key points of her new objective, telling people:

> *"I am exploring how to capitalize on my engineering background and passion for incorporating technology into innovative new products. I have spent 12 years honing my strengths. These are my ability to research and analyze the design and usability of new products and my ability to communicate effectively with engineers, designers and customers and solve problems related to functionality. One area that I'm looking at is industrial design. I'm not necessarily looking at becoming a designer, but I'm exploring, perhaps, a liaison role between the client and designer."*

This is the place to start as you prepare to talk about yourself at this juncture. You simply need to add a few more key points.

We'll call this your *stump speech*. You want to have several versions of this stump speech—a short, 30-second one like what you developed in Step 7, a longer, 90-second rendition and a 3-minute version.

Think of this speech as a standard spiel that you will carefully craft and deliver—just like a political candidate—at every whistle stop. You'll adapt, depending on the circumstance, your audience, your goal and how much time you have. Except for a customized tweak and variation of length, the speech should echo the same themes and six key messages in an organized, concise way each time.

Whether you are in a job interview and hear the request, "Tell me about yourself," or are sitting down to pick someone's brain about their industry, the person across from you is wondering six things:

1. Are you a decent person I can trust and would want to hire or refer to people I know?
2. Why are you in this situation—that is, wanting a job in a new field?
3. What were you doing before this?
4. What do you know about and what have you done to prepare yourself for this new career?
5. What are your key strengths (your most joyful skills)?
6. What do you want to do now, and how serious are you?

DON'T MAKE THIS DULLSVILLE

You want your stump speech to be conversational and not sound so memorized and rehearsed that it's dull and tedious. Don't write it out word for word. If you do, you'll try to repeat the exact words. And if it doesn't come out exactly right, you'll get flustered and distracted, and you won't make sense. Plus, depending on who you're talking to, you'll need to adapt content. Leaving out a fact or two is not the end of the world. Packing this with relevant information that's drenched with your passion for why you want this new career matters most.

Remember Leonard, the software analyst, who applied for the job at the restaurant? In the first minute he had with the chef who had granted him a 15-minute interview, he told him, "I have no restaurant experience and no culinary skills, but I have more passion, a better work ethic and more desire than anyone you'll bring into this room." He got the chance to tell him more, but passion is what hooked the chef. This led to a four-hour interview.

To create your stump speech, develop an outline that includes chunks of information you plug in or leave out and lets you condense or elaborate, depending on the circumstances. The "chunks" might include:

1. Why you are in this situation—that is, wanting a job in a new field
2. What you were doing before this and, if applicable, are currently doing
3. Your key strengths (most joyful skills)
4. What you know about and what you have done to prepare for this new career
5. What you want now and how passionate you feel about it

Most of this information is in the new career objective you've already created. Let's look at how you might develop this into your stump speech. I'll give you examples of the type of wording and tone that speaks to all five points. Notice how several points can be conveyed in response to one question.

The elements of your stump speech

To create your stump speech, think about all five "chunks" of information you might want to convey.

HOW TO EXPLAIN WHY YOU'RE IN THIS SITUATION—WANTING A NEW CAREER

Remember in Step 2, I asked you to think through and write answers to these questions:

1. Why you want to change careers
2. What specifically hasn't been right about your career
3. How your career up to now has adversely affected your life

Then I had you put all those answers together and summarize the gist of why you want to change careers.

I explained that doing that would give you language to help explain—when the time comes—why you want to change careers. Now is that time.

Despite some of the reasons you wanted to change careers, don't get negative. You might have to tone down what you wrote, probably leaving off how your old career adversely affected your life. But those responses you wrote in Step 2 are where to start for the delicate crafting of your response.

Also, don't badmouth anyone at the last place you worked or get all pissy about things if you were laid off. Just as it is hard for people to understand what you're saying when you're yelling, it's hard for people to see past annoyance, anger and what you really want if you're focused on "what they did to you."

There also seems to be "something hard-wired into humans that gives special attention to negative information," said Kathleen Hall

Jamieson, director of the Annenberg Public Policy Center at the University of Pennsylvania in a *New York Times* article during the 2004 presidential campaign.

She refers to it as evolutionary biology, and "the wariness of our ancestors that made them more likely to see the predator and hence to prepare. The one who was cautious about strange new food probably didn't eat it; they sat back and watched other people die. There's a reason to be hesitant about that which is vaguely menacing."

In meetings with people who don't know you, they will be cautious and hesitant if you seem vaguely menacing by sounding angry or resentful. And since our brains seem to give special attention to the negative, this is not how you want them to remember you.

In this chunk, you want people to understand where you've been and make the case for why you want to make a career change—with the focus on what you want to move toward, not what you want to get away from.

When I first asked Jerry, the operations analyst and sales associate, why he wanted to change careers he said, "I never gave any thought into why I was choosing a career. I just fell into it. I guess I made stupid choices. Then after being in it, I couldn't stand thinking about computers anymore." As the listener, I might empathize. But it doesn't help build his case of what he wants to move toward.

Here's a better response. In this example, Jerry explains why he wants to change careers. But it also makes sense for him to share what he was doing before, plus give insight into his key strengths and what he wants to do next. So in this response, he's answered more than just the question: Why do you want this new career?

"For the last six years I have been an operations analyst and sales associate for a bookstore, where I consulted with customers on their computer hardware and software needs. I enjoyed using my strengths to assess their needs, research, develop trusting relationships and counsel them. I also have applied these skills in another area—with friends and family members who wanted help with diet and exercise—something I'm very interested in. Those experiences reinforced for me how much I enjoy using those skills, but also how interested I am in healthy lifestyles. I have spent extensive time researching healthy lifestyle choices for myself and others, with very positive results. I've done a lot of soul searching and research and decided that I want to apply these strengths to this area I care deeply about: creating a happier life through healthy lifestyle choices.

"So my objective now is to find a position where I can contribute my new education and passion for improving the health and well-being of others, through my strengths to assess, build trusting relationships, clearly communicate information and counsel others."

Notice:

▶ He never got negative or talked about his "stupid choices" or how he hated thinking about computers. He shared facts, and didn't sound like a floundering fool but someone who had put a lot of thought into his choice.

▶ He focused on his strengths and showed how well they could transfer into a new area.

▶ He created a case for how he came up with this next career by emphasizing his strengths, explaining how he had dabbled in this work before and sharing what he cared deeply about.

▶ He ended on a positive note about the future, not by dwelling on the past.

Depending on the situation, he could even give an example of how he has applied his strengths in a new way, by saying something like:

"For example, I assessed the eating and exercise habits of a 32-year-old overweight male friend and developed a diet and weightlifting regimen, advising him at regular intervals. He lost 60 pounds in six months."

Or:

"Applying what I've learned from my self-study, I lost 100 pounds, stopped smoking, and developed a daily exercise regimen and diet that dramatically lowered my cholesterol."

HOW TO EXPLAIN WHAT YOU WERE DOING BEFORE (OR, IF APPLICABLE, WHAT YOU ARE CURRENTLY DOING)

If you haven't covered this point already, you might say something like the following (citing information that could be relevant to your new career):

▶ "For the past 10 years, I've been working in information technology, where I've been a project manager for several software development firms."

▶ "I have 15 years in the financial-services industry, where I've developed a reputation for building trusting relationships and always delivering results in my work as a financial advisor."

▶ "I have been in project engineering in chemical and pharmaceutical manufacturing, where I trained clients on procedures and processes as they started up new plants."

▶ "I have been in sales and sales management, working mostly for commercial and industrial manufacturers who make highly engineered products such as electric motors. Right now, I'm assisting a professor in her research to gain experience into a new career as a researcher while I complete my education."

HOW TO EXPLAIN WHAT ARE YOUR KEY STRENGTHS

If you haven't covered this point already, you might say something like the following examples (citing strengths that are relevant to your new career):

▶ "My strengths include my ability to solve problems related to product performance and mechanics, to train others and explain technical information in understandable language."

▶ "I am very skilled in being a hands-on problem solver when it comes to analyzing technical problems, processes and equipment; researching and presenting scientific data; writing documentation; and developing training curricula."

▶ "My strengths are my ability to motivate and direct others, solve operational problems, conceptualize, plan and develop new projects and build consensus to meet goals."

▶ "My strengths are my ability to plan, coordinate and organize special events, develop efficient operating procedures, envision and oversee the big picture and negotiate complex contracts."

HOW TO EXPLAIN WHAT YOU KNOW ABOUT AND WHAT YOU HAVE DONE TO PREPARE FOR THIS NEW CAREER

"Through my self-study and the coursework I've been taking for the past year, I have developed extensive knowledge about exercise, nutrition, physiology, stress, weight training, strength conditioning and healthy cooking methods. By the end of this year, I will have my personal trainer certification from the American Council on Exercise and be a full-fledged member of the National Federation of Professional Trainers."

HOW TO EXPLAIN WHAT YOU WANT NOW AND HOW PASSIONATE YOU FEEL ABOUT IT

If you haven't covered this point already, you might say something like:

"I am exploring how I can contribute my 10 years of creating successful special events for professional associations into a full-time career. I have loved doing everything from handling logistical issues and publicity to coming up with themes, menus and entertainment—and have developed a reputation for always delivering a memorable experience for people."

The spawning of your stump speech

Go to a quiet place and think through what you'll say. Write an outline using this as your guide and hit the high spots on:

1. Why I'm in this situation—wanting a new career
2. What I was doing before (and, if applicable, am doing now)
3. My key strengths
4. What I know about and what I've done to prepare for this new career
5. What I want now and how passionate I feel about it

Then create three versions to fit approximately three lengths: 30 seconds, 90 seconds, and 3 minutes. It's difficult to predict which version you will use when. Here are some guidelines.

30 seconds, if:

- You're standing up to introduce yourself in a group meeting
- You're waiting in line to introduce yourself to a speaker you just heard
- You just met someone who asks, "What do you do?"

90 seconds or 3 minutes, if:

- You want to give more details on an area that supports a specific point

    For example, if you want someone to know how passionate you are about a career working with animals, you can tell them about the time you rescued a litter of four kittens from the side of the freeway, brought them back to health and found homes for all of them within a week.

    Or if you want someone to see how you developed a reputation as a meeting planner who anticipates and plans for every detail of an event, give an example:

    "I planned and coordinated an annual state convention for 300 attendees, including site location and catering three meals a day. I oversaw transportation, advertising and conference packets. The conference was named the most well-run event in the organization's history."

- You sense someone wants more detail or they ask for it. Elaborate with some of the particulars you prepared in your 90-second or 3-minute version. You might first ask what area they'd like to hear more about.
- You're in a more formal meeting or interview. You can go into more detail in response to the request, "Tell me about yourself." To gauge how much the interviewer wants to know, you can ask, "Is there a particular area you'd like to hear about?"
- You've asked someone to meet with you to get input about your new career direction

At the beginning of the meeting, kick things off by saying, "Let me start by telling you a little bit about myself." Then share the 90-second or 3-minute rendition—as long as it's tight and meaty.

Sample 90-second stump speech

"For the last six years, I have been an operations analyst and sales associate for a bookstore, where I consulted with customers on their computer hardware and software needs. I enjoyed using my strengths to assess their needs, research, develop trusting relationships and counsel them.

"I also have applied these skills in another area—with friends and family members who wanted help with diet and exercise—something I'm very interested in and knowledgeable about. Those experiences reinforced for me how much I enjoy using those skills, but also how much I care about healthy lifestyles. I have spent extensive time researching healthy lifestyle choices for myself and others, with very positive results. I've done a lot of soul searching and research and decided that I want to apply these strengths to this area I care deeply about: creating a happier life through healthy lifestyle choices.

"Through my self-study and the coursework I've been taking for the past year, I have developed extensive knowledge about exercise, nutrition, physiology, stress, weight training, strength conditioning and healthy cooking methods. By the end of this year, I will have my personal trainer certification from the American Council on Exercise and be a full-fledged member of the National Federation of Professional Trainers.

"So my objective now is to find a position where I can contribute my new education and passion for improving the health and well-being of others, through my strengths to assess, research, counsel and build trusting relationships."

Note that in this last part, where he states his objective, he incorporates his Why the World Would Care Statement. (You developed yours in Step 7.) This is that statement that shows how what you might do benefits the world. It's one key reason someone sees value in you for their organization and it shows you understand the purpose of your work.

> *"It's not what you say, it's what they hear."*
>
> **RED AUERBACH**
> former Celtics coach, discussing pregame pep talks

You can have all the credentials, education and know-how for your next career, but if you can't let loose with a little passion, it will be hard to convince people to help you along the way or, eventually, offer you a job. Don't be afraid to express your zeal, through your words and enthusiasm, for what you want to do next and why you want to do it.

Use emotional language. It's okay to look someone in the eye and say, "I love helping the elderly" or "I'm moved to want to sing" or "I feel so strongly about making this change, I've devoted the next year of my life toward getting this education."

But can I trust you?

We've addressed all the questions someone might be wondering about you except one: *Are you a decent person I can trust and would want to hire or refer to people I know?*

As Jerry Della Femina, the advertising man and restaurateur said in a 2005 article in the *New York Times*, "'Let's face it, we're all a little suspicious of strangers.'" Not to mention, the article adds, people you haven't heard from in years.

It goes on to say that Sara Nelson, who had been named new editor in chief of *Publishers Weekly*, "has been getting notes, flowers and gifts from people who suddenly want to catch up with her over lunch or dinner."

You can't blame someone for being hesitant to talk in the first place, let alone suspicious of your intentions.

Whether you are talking by phone or meeting face to face, people will be quick to size you up. They'll be thinking: Do I like this person and want to help? Does this person have genuine intentions, or are they just using me? There's no science to building trust, but you can influence whether someone feels good about you.

Tim Sanders, in his book *The Likeability Factor*, wrote that the four aspects of likeability are:

1. Friendliness
2. Relevance
3. Empathy
4. Being real

How would you rate if we met for the first time?

Friendliness: Would I feel good upon meeting you? Would you make me feel welcome? Do you smile? Are you enthusiastic? Would *you* want to spend time with you?

CHARLIE EXPLAINS HIS MOVE FROM COP TO TEACHER

At the end of Charlie's 23-year career as a police officer, he was exhausted physically, emotionally and spiritually. His work, as he put it, was, "Filled with boredom or the terror of a robbery in progress, rapist on the loose or a murder that just took place . . . where you prayed you would make it home some nights to go to an officer's funeral the next day."

Not exactly good dinner or interview conversation. So instead of sharing such depressing information about why he wants to make a change, he can offer an honest yet more uplifting response:

"I did important work for 23 years as a police officer. At times it was very difficult and took its toll. I'm at a point in my life where I want to do work that gives back to the community, provides hope and makes a difference in a youngster's life. That's why I want to be a teacher."

Relevance: How well would you connect to what I want or need? Would you share information that's relevant to me and to our purpose in meeting?

This is one reason I talk so much about sharing relevant information. Before a job interview, think through what the hiring manager needs and share information about your background that supports that.

In preparing for networking meetings, think through what that person needs to know to be able to give you advice, to understand your background and know that you're a decent human being.

Empathy: Do you have a sense of what I may be going through or what motivates me?

Think through potential objections an employer might have about hiring you and be prepared to address them. Consider what could make them hesitant, such as how serious you are about this change, whether you'll like it and how long you'll stick with it, or whether you'll be satisfied with making less money—if that's the case—or not being the big cheese.

In a networking meeting, acknowledge the fact that the person's time is important and that you appreciate their arranging to meet with you.

Being real: Do you come off as genuine—as Sanders put it, "factual and actual"? Or are you busy trying to impress me in some way?

Don't exaggerate your experience by saying you've done things you haven't or know more about a subject area than you really do. Also, don't negate your own feelings and be disingenuous. For example, you can be excited about this new career while sharing your humanness, saying something like, "I'm thrilled to finally be able to be a nurse—something I've thought about for years. Of course, it's a bit scary starting something new. But I know I'm prepared and ready to take on the challenge."

Don't butter up people you haven't talked to in years because you think they can help you now. People can see right through it. If you want to contact someone you've been remiss in keeping up with, acknowledge your part in not taking the initiative to keep in touch. Tell them you feel bad about how long it's been since you've spoken. And if they do agree to talk, keep the relationship going so you're not in that situation again.

You often hear these skills referred to as "soft skills," and not necessarily considered very important or relevant. Yet, if you ask people what made them hire one person over another, or want to help them in the first place, they will almost always refer to something they can't quite put their finger on. It usually comes down to how someone *feels* about you.

QUESTIONS CAREER CHANGERS MIGHT HEAR

Having created your stump speech, you have covered most of these. Be prepared to respond to them as individual questions:

- Why do you want to go into this field?
- What makes you qualified?
- What were you doing before, and why do you want to leave your old career?
- How can you do something that's so different from your old career?

If you're not prepared, these three questions could throw you:

1. How do you feel about working for someone younger than you?
That's always a possibility at any point in your career. And at this juncture, you've probably anticipated it. So say that, and add that you have much to learn and that you look forward to working with people who have been in this field—no matter what their experience level.

2. How do you feel about starting at the bottom?
That may not necessarily be the case. But if it is, you knew, going into your new career, that that's where you'd need to start. Explain that it comes with the territory, and you look forward to progressing in this new field.

If the question refers to money, you want to handle it like any conversation about salary: Don't discuss it until you've been offered a position.

So you want to say something like: "Being new to this field, I wouldn't expect to be compensated as a more experienced person would be. Based on the experience I do have and my other qualifications, I'm sure that if we both think I'm right for this position, we could agree on a fair salary."

ANOTHER HANDY TOOL

In case you do find yourself in an informal situation or one where you only have about 20 seconds to explain yourself, here's a handy tool that lets you whittle things down to a sound bite.

It's called the "You Know How/What I Do" statement, as described in Paul Karasik's book *How to Market to High-Net-Worth Households.*

In this format, you don't just state what you want to do, but you tell what you want to do in a way that the listener hears a benefit and quickly understands. For example, if you want to be an estate lawyer, you wouldn't just say, "I want to be an estate lawyer."

Instead, here's the statement I helped my client develop. It has two parts. The first part begins: "You know how . . . " The second part begins with, "What I do is . . . "—or in this situation, "What I want to do is . . . "

So the person who wants to be an estate lawyer might say:

"*You know how,* when someone's close relative passes away, the family is overwhelmed with the responsibility of dealing with their finances? *What I want to do is* make sure that the person's wishes are carried out so the family is taken care of and can comfortably move on."

One automatically gets what you are saying. And who knows? The person you're talking to may know someone who can help you.

My client who is focused on advising people about wellness might say:

"*You know how* hard it is to figure out how to eat and exercise right—and stick with it? *What I'm going to be doing* when I complete my education is help people assess their eating habits, exercise regimen and other lifestyle choices and develop a plan for being healthier and happier that they can adhere to."

To come up with your "You know how/what I want to do" statement, first think how someone might use your skills and benefit from them. Then just say it in the way that real people would.

3. You've worked for yourself a long time. Won't that be a problem?

It's smart to anticipate that employers might have some reservations if you've had your own business. Since you've been doing things your way for so long, they could be worried that you won't take direction well or are set in your ways. Be prepared to address that concern, and in some instances, bring it up before it *becomes* an issue. Look for ways to minimize the scary parts of your experience—that is, to employers—and build on your past experience that matters most to them.

As you market yourself, there are three ways to do that:

1. In your resume
Think about how you want the employer to see you. You want to take the focus off your role as a business owner who's used to calling the shots, yet make sure the employer sees the value you bring.

Help the employer see you as a talented professional with a passion for this new career direction. Everything on your resume should support that. Use language that identifies your strongest skills and interests and highlights ways you worked on teams.

2. In your cover letter and initial phone conversations
Tell employers that because you've managed your own business, the skills you've honed and knowledge you've acquired will add value to their business. Aside from the skills needed for the new career, specify other skills you've honed as a business owner that make you desirable. These might include the ability to be decisive, develop budgets, manage others, build relationships and see the big picture while handling details.

Help them see how these skills would transfer well into this new role. Talk about how you were part of a team and relied on others' judgment and expertise. And be sure to point out that at this time in your life, you want to learn from others and bring your skills and value to a business that wants to grow.

3. In interviews
Early on, tell the employer your reason for wanting to change careers and how much thought and energy has gone into your

new career. Tell them how excited you are about contributing your expertise and skills to an innovative, growing company.

Think like the employer and what might worry them. You could say: "It has crossed my mind that you might be concerned about the fact that I've been on my own for the last 15 years. I have given a lot of thought to this step. While I have enjoyed having my own business, I'm clear I want to bring my knowledge and expertise to someone else's business now. I know I have a lot to offer from this experience as a business owner. But I know I can learn a lot. I am very familiar with the daily and long-term issues you deal with and I want to help your business grow and be successful."

Instead of seeing self-employment as a liability, think about how your bundle of skills, knowledge and experience is something someone will want to get their mitts on.

Think through other particular questions you're nervous about hearing and how you'll respond. You're apt to sound less defensive if you've anticipated the objection and worked through your response.

Getting and keeping their attention in the interview

The secret to getting an offer: *Don't sell yourself.*

If you go into an interview thinking, "I gotta get this job" or "I gotta get them to want me," you're working too hard. When trying to sell yourself, you're focused on "what they want to hear" and what you need to do to convince them to want you.

This makes you sound desperate. You're also not thinking clearly. It's hard to ask the right questions and discover if the job is what you want when you're busy trying to sell yourself.

A job interview is a conversation—not a sales call. Most interviewers aren't going into it thinking, "I gotta sell this person on our company so they'll want to work here." Not yet anyway. They're intrigued enough to want to meet, see what you're like and evaluate whether you're the right person for the job. Like you, they will want to cast the company in a positive light. But most important, they will want to get to know you.

Once you get the interview, you should have the same objective as the interviewer: To explore whether this is a good fit while making a positive impression. If you do that well, you're more apt to get to what you want—an offer.

Instead of selling, *influence*.

You do that not by simply telling them what you can do, but *showing them how you can make a difference.*

One of my clients was trying to make a career change from working as a chemical engineer to a role as a trainer in a technical environment. He had trained clients and staff in his former career, but now he wanted that to be his sole focus. He asked me repeatedly whether a company would see his value and understand that his skills were transferable.

It's your job to help them see that, I explained.

You see, a company wouldn't necessarily understand his value or hire him just because his skills are transferable. He would have to build his case. He would need to show them *how* his skills and knowledge could fit into a different role and make a difference to their company. It would be up to him to share specific examples of how his skills had brought about results in the past.

For example, he could talk about how he had developed and presented four training sessions to a company's engineers. This resulted in the early completion of a project, saving the plant $1 million per day in production costs.

He also would need to help them see he had the right mindset, personal characteristics and potential. And he needed to think through an employer's objections and why those need not be a concern. All of that adds up to *influencing*.

Look back at Will, the contractor who specialized in redoing houses, who was so successful at influencing the owner of an ad agency to hire him. He didn't try to sell the man on anything. He thought about the agency's needs and how he could help the owner fulfill those needs. He discussed his credentials, experience and passion for the advertising industry.

OLDER WORKERS CAN BE
HIGH AND MIGHTY

Older workers making a career change offer a strong work ethic, values and maturity that are highly regarded in the workplace. One California career changer in her mid-40s, working in her new field of public affairs, recalled her experience, which highlights the advantages of being an older worker:

> "I have lived in this city for over 20 years. I have friends in different fields who can help me. I have stable priorities. I am more patient. My new boss sheepishly admitted that he wanted a 'mature candidate.' They got a zillion resumes, but were holding out for someone like me. He and the management over him recognized they needed someone who had all that extra seasoning. I started with a fairly junior title and pay, but I'm confident I'll bump up fairly quickly here."

He also gave examples of how he had made a difference. He told his prospective employer: "I developed the strategy and advertising for an issue-driven political campaign. The initial polls had us at about 50 percent of the vote, and after being outspent ten to one by our opposition, we still won by 73 percent of the vote."

In addition, he showed the interviewer how his skills in being a contractor would transfer to an account executive role in his advertising agency.

"I explained how I meet with clients to find out their needs, sell them on my services, develop an estimate and plan, assemble a team of people from different disciplines, manage them and complete the project on time and within budget. That's the essence of what an account executive does in an ad agency."

Will and the owner had five *conversations* about whether they were a good fit for each other. In every conversation, Will influenced this man with his words, demeanor and actions to sufficiently answer the questions on the owner's mind:

1. Can I trust you?
2. Why do you want this new career?
3. What were you doing before this?
4. What do you know about and how have you prepared for this career?
5. What are your strengths?
6. What do you want to do now, and how serious are you?

Woes and Worries

YOUR AGE: DON'T ASK, DON'T TELL

As I said in Step 8, some worry is normal. But don't feed the fear. Now that you're ready to market yourself, be prepared to deal with an objection about "your age" if you hear it.

It's unlikely—but not unheard of—that a concern about your age will be stated in so many words. But if you're worried an employer might give you the brush-off because they think you can't do a job that requires understanding of new technology, be prepared. Create phrases that you'll weave into your communications to demonstrate how up to date and willing you are to learn and lead.

List these as bullet points in your cover letter and resume. Describe yourself as a lifelong learner who understands the value of change to keep the organization competitive. And don't forget to mention how devoted you are to the company's initiatives and how you share similar values.

As I talk to employers in various fields, I hear a shift in how they see older workers. Many understand how focused, loyal and energetic older workers can be. And they realize it's not wise to only recruit younger professionals, since this is a diminishing pool of talent.

OLDER WORKER DISADVANTAGE—SORT OF

If you end up working in an industry that is typically populated by younger workers, one drawback, said a 40-something career changer, is that "you have no one to eat lunch with. You can't hang out with the 25-year-olds at your career level and the execs your age are senior management. I talk about my kids too much and they are not much younger than some of my colleagues!

"I also have holes in my basic skill set and have to work hard to understand some basic tools. I have had to play catch-up on some computer skills—Excel, for instance. In my past career, I basically had a secretary who would take care of stuff like that."

But because she is physically fit and has a youthful outlook, she said she fits in, "although I am older by five years than anyone else here, including senior management." Even so, she said, "The people I work for are great, and the work that I have done has literally grown the business and they are very happy with me."

Other factors also make experienced workers valuable. Bruce Cox, partner with Callaway Partners in Atlanta, said the growing accounting field in particular will be utilizing experienced professionals in nontraditional accounting jobs. Many ex-CFOs and controllers are now being employed by companies like his: "We execute a hybrid fixed and flex-staff consulting model, which enables us to adapt to large-scale client needs while maintaining service and quality."

A smart employer who sees your value (because you've explained it) won't ask about or be deterred by your age. And you don't need to talk about it because, after all, it's irrelevant.

THE KINDS OF COMPANIES TO SHOP FOR

Since you hear mostly about large companies—the ones with the big buildings you drive by—you'll have a tendency to equate them with more jobs, stability, pay and benefits.

Big companies may take up more room. But with the many small companies that exist, the jobs—even though fewer per company—add up to a good number. According to the Small Business Administration's (SBA) Office of Advocacy, small firms represent more than 99.7 percent of all employers, employing more than half of all private-sector employees and generating 60 to 80 percent of new jobs annually.

Although the SBA defines a small business as one with less than 500 employees (depending on the industry), I find companies over 100 employees can be like big companies, so I'd use that smaller figure—less than 100—to define a small business. If you want to work for a small company, this number is probably closer to what you have in mind.

So where should you focus your job search? First, look at the pros and cons of working for a small vs. a large company and decide what's best for you. Then look for companies—big or small—that are raring to grow and succeed.

Innovation is the name of the game when it comes to survival and growth. Find the healthy companies. These are the ones who are innovative, have business savvy, are poised to grow, have state-of-the-art technology and understand and deliver what their customers want.

Instead of looking for the greatest number of opportunities, look for large or small companies that are doing their work in the most innovative way.

Your resume: Don't tell all, do show what's relevant

Just as you've done in preparing to talk about yourself, you want to create a marketing document that positions you as you want others to see you: as someone with past experience to build on and the skills, knowledge, interest and personal characteristics to do this new work.

So, as you did in talking about yourself, list information on your resume that's *relevant* and supports your new objective.

Does that mean you don't list every single job you've had? Possibly. Does it mean you leave off the first 10 years of your work life? You might.

You need to decide whether the information is relevant and supports your new objective. It might be important to show that you worked during a period, but the details aren't relevant to what you want to do now. So you could list the jobs, but not go into detail.

Be careful not to cross the line between persuasive marketing and lying. Lying includes misrepresenting the number of years you've done something, exaggerating or taking credit for something you didn't do.

"Most lying is pragmatic," said Professor Leonard Saxe of Brandeis University, a guest on the NPR radio program *Talk of the Nation*. The more situational pressure people are under, he said, the more apt they are to lie. Sometimes people believe that everybody else is cheating. In the case of resumes, people may think that everybody else is inflating their background. So to be competitive, they think, they have to do it as well.

Here's the rule: Never lie.

You do, however, want to develop a marketing tool that will help the reader understand your potential to be successful in this new career. Creating a document that gives a detailed history of every job you've had in your life will probably not do that effectively.

If, though, you don't want to leave gaps, make a statement on your resume that explains what you've been doing. For example, let's say you are making a change from database analyst to sales, and while in transition you've had several jobs unrelated to either role. Include the line, "Other positions include temporary administrative jobs." Or, if early in your career you were in public relations, you might say, "Prior positions include . . . " and list those jobs.

You don't need to stretch the truth or lie when looking for your new career position. If you do lie and you're found out, it can make someone wonder what else you're hiding. Worse, if you've lied to get a job and an employer finds out, you risk losing the job you worked so hard to get.

Remember, if you're conducting a strategic job search, you—not your resume—are what people see first. Your resume is a document you either leave behind or use when applying for a job through traditional channels. It's still a necessary and important tool in this process. But make it work for you.

As you're creating this new resume, keep your goal fixed in your mind: to show others you have past experience and skills (and possibly knowledge), personal characteristics and interests, *and* newly acquired knowledge that help qualify you for your new career.

You do that on your resume by:

▶ Making a point to state your transferable skills, so that others will be able to clearly see that you have this body of skills that can be used elsewhere

▶ Making it easy for the reader to see your knowledge in a bullet-point format

▶ Including phrases that tell about your personal qualities, such as "reputation for being empathetic and caring," "known for tactful handling of sensitive situations and getting to the bottom of a problem" or "known for ability to quickly build trust and put people at ease"

▶ Including relevant volunteer experience that enhances your credentials

▶ Listing achievements from your past with concrete results that illustrate how your skills and knowledge made a difference—and can do so in this new career

Here are some examples:

A nurse who wanted to show her skills, knowledge, and hands-on experience in promotions and communications included these achievements:

- Assisted in development of a documentary film that has been viewed by 9 million students and contributed to a reduction in traumatic injuries.

- Conceived idea for partnership with a local television station that created multimedia promotional campaign, raising over $300,000 in corporate sponsorships.

- Planned and implemented strategies to fund promotional campaigns that resulted in over half a million dollars in corporate donations and in-kind media.

The following person, who came from a nonprofit background, wanted to demonstrate his strategic-marketing and planning skills, so he listed this achievement on his resume:

- Developed and implemented a communications strategy that resulted in passage of $90-million tax levy.

One client of mine wanted to illustrate her training skills, so she included this achievement:

- Trained team of designers on Macintosh operating procedures and software that allowed company to use vendor's digital information and significantly enhanced graphic presentations.

This executive, who wanted to demonstrate his leadership ability and skills in motivating workers, made these points:

- Created work environment and culture that resulted in highest-rated employee satisfaction surveys within corporation in communications, teamwork and supervision.

- Developed creative recruiting techniques and rewarding work environment that increased staff 400 percent within two years and maintained high productivity level while averaging 15 percent attrition rate, compared to 30 percent industry average.

Here are two sample resumes I created for clients who were making career changes that show how to incorporate the points I just listed. Names and places are fictional.

Jerry Canary

25990 Ameritas Way
Larchmont, New York 10538
914/922-2222

PROFILE

Certified personal trainer with ten years experience working with the public in retail and computer software consulting. Reputation for being customer focused and committed to discovering the core of a problem and working toward tangible results. Strong interest in physical fitness, healthy eating and nutrition, with a passion for improving the health and well-being of others. Skilled in advising others by applying proven strengths to:

- Identify and solve problems
- Develop trusting relationships
- Motivate and lead others
- Create processes and plans
- Clearly communicate concepts and benefits of a solution

Extensive self-study, formal education and exposure to:

- Health care
- Smoking cessation
- Massage
- Exercise programs including cardiovascular, running, aerobics and backpacking
- Safe and effective strength conditioning and use of exercise equipment
- Weight training for beginners to intermediate
- Sports including distance running, golf and softball
- Nutrition and diets including vegetarianism, proper protein consumption, vitamins and calorie consumption
- Stress-reducing activities
- Ergonomic work space, posture and physical therapy
- Cooking methods and food safety

Business knowledge encompasses:

- Customer service
- Business plans
- Small-business development and operations
- Retail pricing and merchandising

Operations Analyst/Sales Associate   1996–2006
Fordham University Bookstore, Computer Department, Tarrytown, New York
Assessed thousands of customers' needs for computer hardware and software, conducting one-on-one consultations with students for university bookstore. Acted as resource for faculty, students and academic departments on networking and computer-related issues. Researched computer hardware and software compatibility, performance and price. Developed e-commerce Web site, brochures and in-store promotions and provided systems support.

**SELECTED ACHIEVEMENTS
RELATED TO HEALTH AND WELLNESS**

- Assessed 32-year-old overweight male and his eating and exercise habits, developing healthy eating plan and weight-lifting regimen that resulted in a 60-pound weight loss in six months.
- Advised 23-year-old female, creating diet based on portion management, food choice and exercise program that led to her achieving and sustaining a 25-pound weight loss for nine months.
- Acted as support system for 32-year-old male to help maintain desired weight through exercise and healthy eating habits during stressful life changes.
- Acted as informal resource to dozens of people on basic diet, weightlifting and aerobic exercises, identifying and developing new behaviors that have led to healthier lifestyles and mindsets for long-term results.
- Participated in half marathons in Lansing, Michigan, San Francisco, California and Boston, Massachusetts.

EDUCATION

Bachelor of Arts, The Ohio State University 1996

Personal Trainer Certification, American Council on Exercise 2006

Continuing education at Stoneworth Community College including coursework in physiology, nutrition, vegetarianism, smoking cessation, weight training, massage, relaxation training and stress management

PROFESSIONAL AFFILIATIONS

Member, National Federation of Professional Trainers

Doug Foodover
1288 Medford Road
Cleveland, Ohio 44118
216/524-4444

PROFILE

A resourceful professional with extensive experience creating successful events for professional associations. Fifteen years in the legal field, with specific expertise in negotiations and contracts.

Reputation as a meeting planner who always ensures an enjoyable, hassle-free experience, utilizing strengths to:

- Plan, coordinate and organize special events and meetings
- Develop efficient operating procedures
- Troubleshoot and solve logistical problems
- Envision and oversee the big picture and details

Knowledge encompasses:

- Project management
- Gourmet cooking and wine
- Tours, transportation and travel arrangements
- Promotions
- Audiovisual equipment
- Fundraising
- Catering
- Conference planning
- Menu development and food presentation, including banquets and buffets
- Working with facilities and hotel managers, convention centers, travel agents, caterers and destination management firms
- Booking speakers

EXPERIENCE

Meeting Planning Experience:

Mediation Lawyers Association   2006
Meeting Planner
Planned and coordinated state convention for 300 attendees, including site location, catering and entertainment. Negotiated in-season room rates and coordinated marketing, registration, logistics, room assignments and local and air transportation. Developed conference packet including maps and sponsorship and conference materials.

- Cited as the most successful, highly attended and well-run event in the history of the organization.

<u>Midwest Lawyers Association</u>   1995–2006
Meeting Planner
Oversaw planning of seven conventions for regional professional association for up to 600 attendees in Midwest, Southwest and Northeast
locations. Arranged for convention facilities, planned agenda, and scheduled speakers, including celebrity guests. Arranged travel for speakers
and oversaw entertainment, awards, catering and registration.
- Negotiated room rates and resort, Internet, ground
  transportation and audiovisual services fees that reduced
  meeting costs and increased association's conference
  revenue by 10 percent over previous year.

<u>Midwest Lawyers Association</u>   2002
Meeting Planner
Planned three-day special event for regional organization for 500
attendees. Arranged banquet facilities and hotel accommodations
for out-of-town guests, keynote speaker and entertainers. Oversaw
registration and publicity, planned meals and family events.

<u>Legal Rights Association</u>   1998
Meeting Planner
Planned educational seminar, tennis tournament, and other recreational
activities in Miami, Florida for 150 attendees. Worked closely with desti-
nation management company to coordinate facility and hotel booking.
Oversaw catering, educational materials, speakers and marketing.

Legal Experience:

<u>Carlson and Gahle, LLP, Cleveland, Ohio</u>   1991–present
Attorney
Negotiate and draft legal documents and contracts and counsel legal
and management staff for full-service law firm.

EDUCATION & CERTIFICATIONS

Certified Meeting Professional 2006

J.D. Quinnipiac College School of Law 1990

B.A. University of San Diego 1985

Continuing education includes: Event Management . . .
Hospitality Details . . . Hotel Operations and More . . .

PROFESSIONAL AFFILIATIONS

Member, Meetings Professional International
Member, Professional Convention Management Association
Member, International Special Events Society

Getting experience when you don't have any: Create it

Judith was making a career change from the entertainment industry to public relations at age 43. It was "in the wake of the high-tech bust—which had cost a lot of jobs in the public relations field. I couldn't figure out why anyone would hire me, when they were laying off experienced and tested employees."

A friend of hers in the public relations field asked his colleagues if they could use her help—as an intern. Everyone he asked expressed interest. "It turns out the firm that hired me had some internal programs they wanted to launch but couldn't afford to take anyone off of billable work," she said. "So the idea of getting in someone who had writing and strategic skills virtually for ten dollars an hour was kind of a no-brainer for them."

Within months, she was working on client accounts. "Six months after I started, someone quit at the senior account executive level and they offered me the job."

Besides working for little pay, "Having a friend who is well connected is one of those advantages that we older workers have." She had worked as a volunteer with this person who had observed her skills when they served on committees together. Then he hooked her up with the company. "Offering myself as an intern turned out to be a good strategy," she said.

As you can see, not all internships are through formal programs associated with universities. You can contact employers directly and give them a proposal to work for a certain amount of time in order to gain desired specific experience.

You could offer to work for free or at a lower wage—anywhere from weeks to months. When you set up your arrangement, make it clear you hope this leads to a permanent position.

Think of Leonard, the chef who, at three different times, either worked for free for three to four weeks or for a low wage to gain experience or prove himself. He accomplished both—and his efforts led to a new career.

This situation is different from a traditional internship, which is closely monitored and has specific learning goals. Sometimes you're paid, sometimes you're not. Check out a source like the National Internship Directory for more information on companies that offer traditional internships.

Most likely, if you approach a large company with this working-for-free idea, they won't know how to handle it. But you'll probably be welcomed with open arms at nonprofit organizations, entrepreneurial companies and business incubators. Incubators are where start-ups and fledgling firms share office space and services. They offer a nurturing environment for mostly light manufacturing and service firms or people developing new products.

You not only get experience, but you also show an employer you're willing to do whatever it takes to make their company a success. You might even end up with a job. Look for companies with problems you can help solve. Then make them an offer they can't refuse.

Volunteering is also a way for you to gain experience and for others to see you in action. You get a taste of what an environment is like—and whether you like it. Also, by being there at an organization, you're more apt to hear about job openings.

While you're working in the environment you want to be in, you may be offered the opportunity you have been hoping for. Remember Aliza, the Internet consultant who approached the news director of Wyoming Public Radio about training her as a radio producer for no pay? She then volunteered to participate in a roundtable discussion for Wyoming Public TV. A few months later, the program director, who had seen her in action, asked her if she wanted to produce a documentary TV series.

WHEN YOU DON'T HEAR BACK

It can be easy to feel rejected and crazy with self-doubt when people don't return your calls and e-mails. It is not excusable behavior on the employers' part, but it's the norm.

Someone's lack of response may have nothing to do with you. The job you were discussing could have been put on hold. Your contact may have gotten sick, or be overwhelmed with work or the interview process. Or they're uncomfortable giving bad news.

Other times, something you may have said or done before or after an interview could have turned them off. You may never know.

When I ask employers why they don't call back, one told me, "It's like dating. If you're interested, you call back; if you're not, you don't call back. If another date falls through and you're left high and dry, you call back the second choice."

Another employer told me if a person sounds desperate in a letter or phone call, spells his name or company name wrong, or laces his letter with typos, "I don't respond." After an interview, he said, "I may not respond because I'm still evaluating the field of applicants and don't have time to be distracted. Or I'm still evaluating the person and don't want to mislead them or get their hopes up."

You don't control how someone responds. So do what you can to influence it. After you've met with a person, always ask if you can call back by a certain date to follow up. Don't give up if your first attempt or two to connect is ignored. Be persistent without being a pest; it underscores how much you want the opportunity. And make sure everything you send is in tip-top shape, so you don't give them a reason to nix you.

WHEN YOU'RE THROWN OFF GUARD IN AN INTERVIEW

This could happen if you're asked a question that you aren't prepared for, you don't get a good interviewer or the interviewer even seems hostile. Whatever it is, emotions are running high and you feel like you're going to lose your cool.

It's hard to know exactly what to say in the heat of the moment. But knowing that it's less about words and more about what's going on inside of you will help you stay calm and clear on what to do. To be prepared for a difficult situation is to have the ability to exercise "controlled relaxation."

"Martial artists, yoga practitioners and others refer to this ability to relax mind and body together deliberately at a moment's notice and without thought as 'centering,'" said Bill Withers and Keami Lewis, authors of *The Conflict and Communication Activity Book*. You're not thinking about a strategy, but "allowing the appropriate choice of action or relationship with the other person to emerge." As odd—and risky—as that might sound, here's why it works.

When you're stressed, your brain and body react through "fight" or "flight"—which can make things worse. This means you can either confront (fight) or walk away (flight). You can feel it in your body—your muscles might tense up or your heart beat faster. When you're "centered," you can "send this energy toward a third choice," allowing you to calmly make a split-second adjustment to do the best thing.

CAN RECRUITERS HELP?

The short answer is, Maybe. But for the most part, working with people who want to change careers is not what recruiters do.

Recruiters work for corporate clients who have asked them to find a candidate to fill a very specific slot in their company. Even though a recruiter can potentially help you, it is not their main purpose, said Adam Steinharter, a technical recruiter with Adam Jacobs Associates in San Francisco.

"I work with many Fortune 100 companies and have solid relationships with them," he said. "They come to me with specific needs. Should I receive a position where the manager could accept a lower-level person or someone looking to break into that specific industry, I could leverage my relationship to make that happen."

This reinforces the importance of developing relationships. It doesn't hurt to get chummy with recruiters who can understand what you want and see your potential. But don't expect recruiters to *find* you a job. They don't do that for anyone.

"Recruiters are driven by their client requirements," added Scott Rodgers, owner of the recruiting firm Scott Rodgers and Associates in Indianapolis. And every employer will have a picture of their ideal client—so it makes sense that many of Rodgers's clients ask him to find "candidates that meet the exact vision of what an ideal candidate should be."

At the same time, he said, a good recruiter is a trusted consultant and can present someone with unusual capabilities "that could add so much more to the overall equation."

So yes—spend a little time getting to know good recruiters. But remember: In the end, as Steinharter said, "I need to satisfy my client, since they pay the bill."

What's a Rabbi to do?

Rabbi Edgar Weinsberg wondered how to go about looking at his next career when the synagogue he had worked at for 21 years merged with another one. As he prepared to move to Florida, he said he had thought about "editorial work, being a hospital chaplain or volunteer director, or working for a nursing home." I suggested he start by looking at his most joyful skills and what he knew and cared about most.

He had written and delivered speeches, taught, counseled and led people, raised funds and spearheaded solutions to community problems. He knew about the Bible, Talmud, theology, pastoral psychology, rabbinical literature, Jewish history, law and tradition, Hebrew, interfaith relations, counseling and volunteers. He had a doctorate in gerontology.

I asked him to think about where he wanted to contribute this body of skills and knowledge. Did he want to work with older people now? If so, what institutions or groups exist that deal with the elderly? If teaching appealed to him, what subjects did he care about and where would he find the students? What colleges, theological seminaries and private schools existed in the area where he was moving? What other institutions could use his background? I suggested he do research on who promotes interfaith relations—an area he was interested in.

While he researched his new direction, I advised him to present himself as a skilled professional and a spiritual leader, with expertise in religious law and tradition and with specific skills and interests. Talking to others would help him think of new roles. And although I probably didn't need to tell this to a wise rabbi like him, I reminded him that the solution often presents itself in the process of discovery.

To practice "centering," they suggest you find your physical center, about three inches below your navel. Stand with your feet shoulder-width apart and take a deep breath, pulling your shoulders up toward your ears. Drop your shoulders as you breathe out. Imagine muscular tension running like water from every part of your body.

Take the fingertips of one hand and lightly touch your center point. Breathe in and out to help feel where your center point is and remember it. Relax and smile as you breathe. As you focus on your center, let yourself breathe as naturally as if you weren't paying attention to it. As you breathe in, say quietly to yourself, "Breathe in," and as you breathe out, say, "Breathe out."

The key is to notice when you've been knocked off center. As you learn to relax your mind and body together at a moment's notice, you'll learn to trust yourself to do or say the best thing when things get tense.

Do you accept this offer as your next career position?

Because you've gone to a lot of trouble to prepare yourself for your new career, make sure job offers line up with what you have said you want. I have had many clients jump at the first or second offer, only to regret the decision. Nine times out of ten, the first offer is not the right one.

How do you know if it's right? First, go back to Step 2, where you wrote what you *never* wanted to do again. So it's fresh in your mind, rewrite that information here:

_____

_____

_____

_____

_____

_____

_____

GOOD DECISIONS REQUIRE

1. Consideration

Consider facts and your feelings. Don't rush it. Sleep on it. Sit with it. Give a decision the time it requires.

2. Clarity

Know who you are and how you picture yourself. How do you want your life to be? Does this look like that?

3. Courage

It takes courage to say *I want this or that—I'm not happy and am willing to do whatever it takes, to give up everything familiar and start with something new.*

You also defined the criteria that fit your life and future, at the end of Step 4. You described what was most important to your overall life, such as only working 30 hours so you would have time to spend on things you value outside of work. Again, so it's fresh, rewrite that description here:

_____

_____

_____

_____

_____

_____

_____

_____

_____

_____

Now look at the other parts of your career objective:

- Your six most joyful skills
- The types of people you might use your most joyful skills with
- What you know about
- What you care about
- The environment and culture where you'd thrive

How does the offer match up? Will you be doing what you enjoy most with people you want to be around, applying what you know and care about in an environment and culture where you'll thrive? Will you be doing what you said you never wanted to do again? Will the offer give you the flexibility you want so that you can have the life you desire? (This last point is something you can negotiate.)

Up to now, you've been in search of a career that fits who you are. Now the question is, does this particular job within that career match up with your values and personality, the life you want and who you are?

If you're not sure because you need more information about the company, ask if you can talk to other employees. Prepare questions to

GET HELP IF YOU'RE STUCK

After Judith left her career as studio executive for a production company and a cable network for 20 years, she floated around for a year.

"I tried to set up movies as a producer and took on an independent job as a fundraiser. I still loved the business and really didn't want to admit failure by leaving the business. I would read the classifieds and realize that there was literally nothing out there that I qualified for. I went to a career counselor. When I furred out my game plan—and articulated what I wanted and how I wanted to get there—it was like I got on a bullet train. It took less than a month for me to get my internship."

find out if the place is a good fit, including whether there is anything about this company new people are "surprised" to learn about.

Make sure you take a tour of the company to see how it feels. Ask people outside the company what they know about the firm and if they've heard what it's like to work there. You might look into working as a temporary employee or consultant first, to test the waters.

You've come far to discover work that uses your strengths, challenges you, is meaningful, fits your values and personality and fits the life and future you want to create. Does this opportunity do that?

Happy endings and how you can get there too

W hether you are at the beginning stages, halfway through the first eight steps or ready to market yourself, you're pretty much on your own. You will have friends, family and associates cheering you on. You may even have a career coach. But they're not the ones doing the hard work—making the calls at eight in the morning to set up meetings, writing e-mail and follow-up letters at ten o'clock at night and conducting research on weekends when everyone else is out having fun. Yes, there *will* be times when you feel alone and doubt may creep into your head. This is part of the process.

Remember in Step 8, when I asked if this felt like the right thing to pursue—even if you didn't know exactly how it was going to turn out—even though you may be inconvenienced, uncomfortable and scared at times? Then I asked you to write out and post the following in a place you see every day:

"I know in my heart this is the right thing to do."

That was your declaration that this is what you want, you are going after it with vigor and nothing's going to stop you. You were saying, "I resolve to go through this process and face the challenges along the way."

Although he doesn't describe it quite like that, you did what Robert Fritz, the author of *The Path of Least Resistance,* calls making a primary choice. From there, you may have rearranged your life, ended something or started something new. You were making new, strategic *secondary* choices, as Fritz put it, to support your primary choice.

Once you make this primary choice, "convenience and comfort are not ever at issue, for you always take action based on what is consistent with your fundamental choice," he wrote.

Then why do you feel inconvenienced and uncomfortable at times? Granted, some activities you have chosen to undertake can be time consuming, even a pain. You may be uncomfortable picking up the phone to ask people for help. As I shared at the beginning of this book, you will feel discomfort. At times, irritated. Itchy about how things will turn out. All of that is to be expected—not avoided.

Aside from this being a valuable time for you to learn about yourself and develop who you are becoming, there also will be times when you will need to draw upon that statement you fiercely declared from the bottom of your heart. It will not only help keep you going through the rough spots, but also will keep you focused on why you are doing this hard work.

It's nice to have as much help as possible in this process. So in addition to this important tool, I want to give you some other structures you can surround yourself with. These include daily, weekly and monthly activities and support to help you stay on plan. They are a mix of philosophical and concrete structures.

Before we get to them, there's one more thing to know. From the beginning of this process, everything you've done has been about *creating* a career that fits your life and who you are. You aren't done creating yet. As you waiver, grapple with your fears and stumble through these tough moments, as Fritz suggested, "Rather than asking, 'How do I get this unwanted situation to go away?' you might ask, 'What structures should I adopt to create the results I want to create?'"

Here are some ideas—in the form of beliefs and actions—that you can adopt to *create* the results you want:

HOLDING THE BELIEF

Shift from trying to control things to *allowing* things to happen.
You don't control anything anyway. So instead of trying to force things to happen or move faster than they are, be receptive to what comes to you.

Focus on gaining patience and endurance as you go through the process.
This will help you develop resilience. Resilient people "usually become stronger when the pressure increases," said William Atkinson, author of *Eliminate Stress from Your Life Forever*. Think of the metaphor of liquid mercury, "which exerts stronger and stronger opposing pressure as more pressure is placed on it."

Walk around with your new goal in your head, paying attention to the clues and guidance that come your way.
When my client Jerry told a few close friends about his vision to help others develop healthy lives, they reminded him of times in their lives when he had advised and motivated them to achieve their goals. This inspired him more, and he told me, "Wherever I go, I keep getting messages that this is the right thing."

Embrace with all your might your belief that this is the right thing to do.
This will draw to you the resources you need: people, information and opportunities.

Remind yourself that things are shifting in this process. Although it may sometimes be painful, it helps to remember there is an end goal. If you've ever had braces, you know what I'm talking about. I got mine when I was 10 years old, and still remember the visits to the orthodontist. Every couple of weeks, he'd adjust the wires as the teeth shifted. I left with my entire head throbbing, tight and full of pressure. Within a few hours, the feeling dissipated. Throughout the two years I had them, I kept thinking about the nice straight teeth I'd have at the end. And when the braces came off at the end of sixth grade, I had those perfectly straight teeth I had envisioned.

Ignore statistics.
Some months unemployment inches up two tenths of a percent. Other months it holds steady. What does that have to do with you and your career change? Whether it's doom and gloom data or good news—nothing.

When you're making a switch, in good or not-so-good economic times, you have to convince an employer that, even though you've never done this exact job, you've got the right attitude and passion, the drive and willingness to learn and make a difference, and the skills and background that will transfer well into this field.

For the most part, when you make a career change, you don't get hired for the experience you have in your new field—because you probably don't have much, if any. It's about proving you're the right person for the job, even without the experience.

People get hired in all kinds of economies because they bring measurable value to a company and can demonstrate it. Potentially, even if a company doesn't have its hiring shingle out, if you add value to the company, *every* company is hiring.

DOING THE DEEDS

Do things that will help you crystallize your idea or support it in some way when it comes to fruition.
I once heard an interview on NPR with actor John Lithgow discussing his belief that there's nothing creative about just sitting around. Advising actors just starting out, he said, "Forget about the job . . . and try to invent something that's all yours. Write something, produce something, direct something, do something that you're in control of . . . I promise you will never get a chance to complete this, because somebody will hire you to act. But meantime, you haven't been waiting around for it. You had something to keep you going."

I urged my client Jerry to create tip sheets he could eventually use with people he'd work with. The sheets might capture, for example, the seven steps to eating right or a way to track a person's weekly food consumption or chart their weight-loss progress. He did this, and he was on his way to creating some of the tools he'd use in his new career. And just as Lithgow predicted, he had to put it aside—for now—as ideas and opportunities started coming his way.

Another development occurred when Jerry was taking a chemistry course at his local university to gain some of the knowledge he wanted for his new career. His professor told him that he would make a good tutor for other chemistry students.

"I took him up on his offer!" he wrote me. "I'm tutoring five students this term. It doesn't pay much, but it's nice to be out of the house, doing something I like to do—namely helping people. So that's been very rewarding." It was also giving him more experience for his new career when it came to fruition.

Have a nice nag buddy.
Ask someone close to you help you stay accountable. They might send you e-mail or call you once a week to check in and gently nudge you on how things are going. Talk to them often so they know what you're

working on, and give them permission to ask, "Did you follow up with so-and-so? How did your meeting with so-and-so go?"

If you're working with a career coach, you can ask this person to play that role. I had a client in Europe who I only spoke to every six weeks. She was still working in her career as an art director and felt she'd just drift back to her day job and lose focus on her new career goal without feeling as if someone was hanging in there with her.

So after each phone meeting, I'd summarize actions she'd take over the next 45 days and e-mail them to her. Within two weeks or so, I'd send her an e-mail to ask how that discussion with someone went and how far along she was on the proposal she was writing. If she ran into obstacles, she'd e-mail me about those and I'd throw out some ideas on how to move forward.

Develop a schedule to be disciplined and productive with your time.
Whether you're working at a full-time job in a company while trying to make this change or working for yourself, create a schedule, setting aside times when you do nothing but your career-change activities. You can, for example, set aside Sunday afternoons from 1 to 4 and Wednesday evening from 7 to 10 as your time to focus solely on things related to your new career.

Jerry was working for himself in his apartment and as a result was alone most of the day. The hours dragged on. When he told me how unproductive he was getting, we looked at how he could be more conscious about how he planned his day. He decided to schedule his exercise at the gym and studying in the morning and his job in the afternoon. It may sound like a minor thing, but when we spoke next, he said that doing that had improved his mood, outlook and productivity.

Program reminders into your Palm Pilot, computer, phone or other electronic gizmo.

Establish a system to remind yourself when it's time to send a follow-up note to someone you said you'd contact in two weeks. Or mark the date on your calendar.

Track your progress daily, weekly, monthly and about every three months.

At the end of each day, take a few minutes to notice what you accomplished:

> Who did you talk to?
> What did you learn from that person, and where does
>   that take you next?
> What new information did you learn from an article or
>   book that helped you get clearer or move forward,
>   or is something you can act on?
> Did you decide anything new or make a new commitment?
> Who got to know you better today and is now a cheerleader?
> Did you have any new revelations, ideas or breakthroughs?

Looking at all the ways you moved forward today, note what you need to do to make the most of them.

At the end of every month, take stock of what you have accomplished over the last 30 days. For a broader picture of your progress, do the same thing at three months.

When I work with career changers, it is easier for me to see their progress than it is for them. I've got a bird's-eye view. I saw Jerry go from being insecure, frustrated and stuck to confident, inspired and enthusiastic, with a clear purpose in mind, in less than six months. Then he would hit a bump and forget where he was when we started. He'd only see the moment in front of him with all his doubt and questions overtaking him, wondering if he was getting anywhere. So I would pull out my notes and point out where he had been two months prior.

"Remember when you were fixated on not knowing how this was going to turn out and you were spending eight hours alone in your apartment? Then you began making phone calls and got out of your funk. And then you were all freaked out about the fact that you didn't know enough of the basics. Here you are, six months later, and you've taken two courses in physiology and nutrition and passed with flying colors. You've honed down the programs you'll take to get your training certificate and you're enrolled in cooking classes for the fall. Instead of feeling overwhelmed with your day job, you've whittled down that time to 20 hours a week and you're doing fine financially."

"Oh yeah, I guess you're right," he'd say. "I really have achieved a lot." Soon he was back on track and moving forward.

If you're not working with a coach, you need to do this for yourself. Put it on your daily and weekly to-do list and mark your calendar every three and six months to review and track your progress. Keep a journal and write how things are going.

Be sure to reward yourself for progress—anything from splurging on a latte with a friend to a nice dinner out. Feeling you have accomplished something gives you a sense of control.

Keep supportive people in your life.

If you have a naysayer relative or coworker in your midst, it's probably best to keep your activities to yourself.

Supportive people are the kind you feel comfortable sharing your feelings with. They may be striving for similar things and understand what you're going through. They could be a resource or just be there when you need someone to talk to.

Surround yourself with words that inspire you.

Tape messages on your wall, mirror, phone and refrigerator or in your car and wallet, and read the words of others that keep you inspired. When I received this letter from a reader in Utah in 2004, I realized how much this matters. She wrote:

"Thank you for your inspiring columns I read in the St. George, *Utah Spectrum*. I am 52 with a Bachelor's degree in anthropology. For

> *"Chance favors the prepared mind."*
>
> **LOUIS PASTEUR**

almost 10 years after getting my degree I diddled around. Because of my own personal demons I never went to graduate school . . . whatever excuses I gave myself. I have been an RN for 19 years. It has been a respectable way to make a living. I always envied people who really loved their jobs. Recently I decided to do something that I have been wanting to do for 10 years. At first I had all the excuses again—another bachelor's degree? What in the world will I do? It will cost a fortune!! I'll be 58 by the time I'm done and paying off school loans 'til I'm in the grave!!

"I have started back to school yet again, to pursue a BS degree in geology, and then hopefully a master's. I feel like I am reembarking on a journey I started 30 years ago. The subject enthralls me—over the years I have bought geology textbooks just to read. This summer I am taking remedial algebra and more . . . It will take at least four years to acquire a BS. My goal is to have my own geology guide company. As I was enrolling back in April, the newspaper carried your article, 'Don't let excuses destroy your dreams for the future.' It has been taped to my refrigerator since and I frequently glance at it. Today the newspaper carried your article, 'Changing careers requires a high-achieving, goal-driven attitude to succeed.' I felt I must write to you, especially since I am facing two more years of math classes!! Thank you for your inspiration and direction.

"P.S. Southern Utah University is a 40-mile drive from my house every day, then I drive back down to St. George (53 miles) and do part-time home health nursing, then home. It is about 100 miles round trip every weekday. But it is worth every inch."

Here is one of the articles the reader refers to:

CHANGING CAREERS REQUIRES A HIGH-ACHIEVING, GOAL-DRIVEN ATTITUDE TO SUCCEED

If you are bound and determined to live up to your full potential and changing careers is the way to do it, be prepared to become a high achiever. This is someone who won't settle for less, pushes the limits and is driven by goals that others think aren't attainable.

High achievers are "constantly stretching their minds, wills and bodies to surpass their limitations," said John R. Noe, author of *Peak Performance Principles for High Achievers*. They set *high goals*—ones that are so far beyond their grasp they must have help to reach them. Their goals are personal—something they want for their own reasons—and timely at that point in their life.

You will need to be a high achiever to change careers, because a lot of people will think what you're trying to do isn't doable. You'll run into obstacles and you'll have to sacrifice something—maybe a lot.

If you're wondering whether you have what it takes to be a high achiever, in order to make a career change or achieve another "high goal," here are some of the questions Noe said to consider:

1. What are you willing to invest?

The energy, time and effort it takes to be a high achiever are enormous. When people tell me they want to make a career change, they often ask, "How long will this take?" My answer is always the same: "As long as it takes."

It's not that you don't have the right to ask. But to become a high achiever, Noe said, you must answer this question: "What are you willing to invest?" with, "I am willing to invest whatever it takes."

2. How much are you willing to endure?

Adversity will dog your every step, he said. "Those who have what it takes to become high achievers learn to endure whatever difficulties they encounter, and they transform difficulties into opportunities." So to this question, the high achiever replies: "Whatever I must endure!"

3. What are you willing to give up?

Most of us are used to having what we want to be comfortable. But when you decide to be a high performer, you must "constantly be willing to give up momentary pleasures and reach for your long-term goals," said Noe.

You may need to give up things that cost you more money than you can afford while going back to school or doing an internship—whatever it is that will help you reach your long-term career goal.

4. Are you willing to start where you are?

You can always get where you want to go, said Noe, providing you're willing to start from where you are. And your high goal can only become real when you're willing to take the first small step. Take, for example, my client who wants to make a career change to the field of industrial design. She realizes she first needs to learn about plastics and manufacturing to be considered for the type of job she wants. So she's willing to be an intern at a company to gain the experience.

High goals can be reached. But in the process, high achievers don't focus on what they have done, but what they are becoming. Because what's really great, as Noe put it, is the "constant joy of achieving progressively higher intermediate goals in the daily experience of preparation." Not to mention that while you're doing that, you are living up to your full potential.

Happy endings:
Getting through the rough times

One thing that will keep you going is the knowledge that others have gone before you and are happier, more fulfilled human beings as a result. Although unexpected events sometimes occurred and fear rocked their faith, they didn't give up. They looked at their investment of time and energy, listened to their hearts and fanned that spark inside them into a flame. And today they are lighting up their lives and the lives of others.

Here, based on some of the people you've followed throughout these steps, is what other career changers ran into at various points, where they found strength, when they felt their faith being tested, how they stuck it out and what their lives are like now.

BETH ANN, FROM INTERIOR DESIGNER
TO THERAPIST

"After I graduated with my new education, fear struck because the jobs available weren't the ones I wanted. I thought I had made a terrible mistake. I wanted to be in private practice, but I couldn't be until I did my time in community mental-health centers. I worked with male adolescent criminal offenders where I wasn't really help-ing—only writing assessments and going to court, dealing with heartbreaking situations with children in the foster care system, giv-ing kids a half hour of peace and safety. I had to put in my time. I clung to the hope that eventually I'd be in private practice. I had invested so much at that point, I didn't want to give it up. I had a need to make a difference. I believed I would and that it would be OK. And it was.

"Now I work in a practice with two psychiatrists, where there's a lot of respect and concern for the well-being of each other. I'm using my strengths, and doing what I care about. I have a lot of autonomy and get great guidance when I need it. I know I'm truly helping people because they tell me and they get better and leave. It feels like who I am and what I should be doing. This work allows me to be creative internally. It's a different kind of interior design."

LEONARD, FROM SOFTWARE ANALYST TO CHEF

"I had decided I never wanted to wonder, 'What if?' And I had to get over the fact that I liked money, because you don't make it in a restau-rant," he told me.

Even when he made the decision to change careers and gave his two weeks' notice at his well-paying job, he said, "I wasn't absolutely certain. I was going on faith and hope and having this good feeling it was the right thing. I surrounded myself with the blessings of many good people."

"The three most important people in my life were my wife, my aunt and the chef who gave me a chance. My wife was very supportive and was a confidante. My aunt became a confidante I could call on any time I was questioning my decision. And I couldn't have done this without my mentor, the chef."

His advice: Find a mentor and keep friends and family around you who understand what this will take.

"If you want to be great at what you do, you have to give your entire self to it. The people around me understand that. It makes the time we do have together so much more valuable."

Marie, from magazine writer to television producer

After Marie lost her job, she said, "I was depressed at times. But I had gone through worse things. I never cried—not because I didn't want to, but because I knew in my heart I would bounce back and that this was meant to be."

She gave herself time to evaluate what hadn't worked in her career and what she wanted next. She wasn't sure what the next thing would be called, but she would know it when she saw it.

"When I had the interview with the production company for the producer job of the gardening show, it seemed perfect, and I was hired. I can work at home much of the time in my wonderful office. I can walk, write, research, learn and think about gardens, plants and ideas for shows, as well as work with great homeowners. I travel a bit and spend days with a crew of about fifteen creating a gardening television show for a national network. I make more money and generally work fewer hours, except during shoot weeks. I have flexibility over my time and control over my life. In my wildest dreams, I wouldn't have thought I would be doing anything like this.

"As I grow older, I have altered my idea of what success is. No longer do I want to be on the top rung of the ladder. I have learned that I am not ambitious enough to pursue it. My husband, our home, and family and friends are extremely important to me. I value those gifts just as much as a career. Now I have time to spend gardening, homemaking, working in our neighborhood and doing many things I love."

Judith, from movie studio executive to public relations professional

Thinking of pursuing this new direction, she said, "I was petrified. Despite a lot of people telling me I'd be great, it was hard to see this myself. One of my closest friends had seen my work and told me that I would do great in the field and would enjoy it."

Her first job in this new career didn't work out. "I am very grateful for the job, but it turned out not to be a good fit," she said. "When my boss left, I was thrown to the wolves. I was completely demoralized. They didn't see my value."

> *"It is not easy to find happiness in ourselves,*
> *and it is not possible to find it elsewhere."*
>
> AGNES REPPLIER

But she found a new job with a company that "actively looks for people who have life experiences and were literally looking for someone older who could work at a middle level. I am so much happier with the day-to-day of my life. I can see that this field will be a home for me until I retire. This past Christmas was my happiest one in years. It was the first time that I wasn't mired in anxiety over whether I would have a job for the year or whether I would be out the door. I made more money when I was 27. However, I can see that I should be able to get back on track to a six-figure salary a few years down the line."

WILL, FROM HOME RENOVATOR TO ADVERTISING COPYWRITER AND ACCOUNT EXECUTIVE

"Now I get paid for thinking. I get paid for creating things that didn't exist before and to have an impact. I get paid for driving my car because in my car I think about and come up with ideas. I came up with an advertising campaign once on my deck during a barbecue, watching the ribs on the grill. What could be better?"

CHARLES, FROM POLICE OFFICER TO TEACHER

"I had people in my life who cared about me—who encouraged me to find myself, to discover who I was and where I was going," he said. One person "put little nuggets out there in conversations that had to do with teaching . . . I was very scared, wondering would I be good enough?"

He decided to pursue this direction, and had his first experience as a substitute teacher of a first-grade class.

"I had *no* idea what I was doing, but I was reading the class a book on animals in the forest and having the children make the animal sounds. I felt movement to my right and this precious little girl, sucking her thumb, nuzzled up into my lap. I was sold. This was for me.

"I cannot imagine doing anything else. It has changed my life in many ways. It is a profession I feel honored to work in. Parents send their children to be under my care. What a blessing and responsibility.

"It's a job where I feel needed, wanted and respected. When I walk into the lunchroom and they all say, 'Hey, Mr. D,' I wonder where I've been all my life. When a hand goes up to add 4 + 5 + 10 and I see the light go on, when the opportunity arises to talk about racism, maybe, just maybe I can make a difference in a youngster's life by something I say or do. To find the lonely, isolated child, and give some special attention to him or her, if only with an instant wink or shoulder hug. But most important, I am learning who I am."

BETH, FROM ENGINEER TO ENTREPRENEUR, OWNER OF MODERN MOTIVE

Beth came to me frustrated and unmotivated, feeling as if her best skills and abilities weren't being used. Physically, her energy was low. After several months of working with me, she decided to leave her job and focus totally on her career change. Her health and her outlook improved. She followed the steps in this book to a T.

"The number-one thing that kept me going and on track was making sure I had completed my 'homework' before I met with you at our regularly scheduled meetings," she told me.

"Getting professional help was what I really needed. When I attended your question-and-answer session at the bookstore, I realized that I was not alone in my career dissatisfaction. That validated my quest to look for something better. It feels good to know you are not alone.

"I always kept a binder with my assignments organized. The assignments helped me realize that I know more than I thought I did. When I talked with other people, I gained a better understanding of my strengths and interests. I realized I could actually be passionate about something. Every time I stepped out of my comfort zone, something good happened as a result.

"A support system of family and friends is invaluable when your self-esteem is waning. I was lucky to have at least one supportive family member initially (the rest came around later). My husband and friends were also behind me all the way."

You'll recall that Beth is the engineer who wanted to analyze and research products and technology that intrigued her and were aesthetically designed. She did a lot of soul-searching and research and concluded she wanted to apply her skills by communicating with customers who, as she put it, "used and cared about everyday, functional products that looked cool."

She also wanted to build on her curiosity and interest in digital technology and stylishly designed, customizable products and the other things she cared about: color, aesthetics and ergonomics. When she was looking for employment at a company, she sought a role where she could track emerging technology and help deliver it to others in the form of cool, everyday products.

"After doing the networking and hard work looking for employment at a firm, I had done even more self-reflection. I really didn't think a nine-to-five job suited me. I'm much happier in an environment where I have control, one in which I am only accountable to myself. I spent most of my life trying to be accountable to others and it never brought me happiness."

Just shy of a year from the time we began working together, she launched her own business, Modern Motive. As the description on her Web site reads, the business "is driven by life and love. A desire for making everyday tasks easier and more fun . . . Our products embody an awareness of style . . . We look to technology and ingenuity to propel us through an evolving era of needs. We look for freshness, reinterpretation and creativity in functional forms . . . "

Doesn't this sound just like Beth? She really has achieved the objective she described to people early in the process: to "explore a liaison role between the designer and people who want to buy aesthetically pleasing, stylish, useful products that they use every day."

"Career is a continuous quest for greater harmony between who you are and what you do."

DR. CAROL KACHIER, author

She ended up doing exactly what she had described. But when she was in the midst of exploring, she didn't know what that role would be called or what situation she'd do it in. It turned out, based on the environment and culture where she thrived and how she wanted her life to be, she found it by creating her own business.

"Now I feel like I am the maker of my destiny. I can make it what I want it to be and live with the consequences."

GARY, FROM EXECUTIVE TO COLLECTOR AND SELLER OF GUITARS

When Gary was struggling with whether to give up his corporate job to go full-time into the business of buying and selling high-end and collectible 20th-century guitars, he was encouraged by those who were close to him. And, he said, "Eventually, two sayings brought me to the realization that I had to make a decision: 'A man who has two jobs does neither one well' and, 'If you take the leap, the net will appear.'"

Since then, he said, besides making more money, he has more flexibility and control over his life than in his previous career. "My quality-of-life quotient was elevated substantially," he said. "It's joyous to do something you love."

MERRITT, FROM EXECUTIVE ASSISTANT TO PERFORMER

Merritt is in the process of leaving the corporate world to become a performer. Although doubts sometimes creep in, she said, she stays motivated by her friends—mostly girlfriends—who tell her she inspires and motivates them.

"I want to make a difference in the lives around me. I want to do great things."

To stay on track, she writes down what she believes she deserves. "For example, I write down that I deserve to do creative work for a living. I deserve to be wealthy. I deserve to be successful. I set goals for three months, six months and one year. Every day, every week, every month, I examine what I have done or am doing to reach those goals."

When she gets frustrated, she said, "I spend time with my dogs. Being outside with them and getting back to nature is a good remedy for the effects of getting caught up in things all too human. I also go to the driving range and hit golf balls. It has become a form of meditation for me. You have to focus only on hitting the ball and you can't think about anything else. It clears my head.

"I'm not afraid of being alone, spending time in the 'void,' because that is when I've made my most exciting discoveries. It's my time to play with my imagination."

PHILLIP, FROM LAWYER TO MEETING PLANNER

Phillip is in the process of his career change. When I last spoke with him, he had met with dozens of professionals in this industry and begun to do the coursework to become certified in the field. Based on the positive feedback he received and information he gathered on what his new career would entail, he told me, "I definitely want to be in the industry. I have the background and talent—this is where I need to be!"

He graduated from a three-day course for professional meeting planners, and now the only question is where he will take his talent, experience and enthusiasm for this new career.

JERRY, FROM OPERATIONS ANALYST AND SALES ASSOCIATE TO WELLNESS ADVISER

He is well on his way to completing his education and getting ready to put out his shingle doing exactly what he had described: to improve people's health and happiness by helping them come up with diet, exercise, sleep and stress-management behaviors and attitudes that are right for them. He'll be:

▶ Using his most joyful skills: assessing, advising, motivating, communicating, creating visuals and counseling

▶ Working with people he defined as those he would most enjoy being around: self-motivated people who are unhappy with the way they look and feel

▶ Incorporating his knowledge and new education on diet, nutrition, exercise, stress management, working with the public, small-business development and operations and marketing

▶ Applying what he cares most about: healthy lifestyles, wellness and education

Since he knew he wanted to be in an environment and culture where he'd be challenged to always get better, rewarded for doing a good job and receiving respectful feedback, he concluded he'd best get that by being on his own.

It started out with the gnawing in the pit of his gut that he told me about the first day I met him: "In the back of my mind, I sense there is a path that better uses my personal strengths and one that is more personally rewarding." It evolved into this: "I don't know what to call it, but I really want to improve the health and well-being of people."

Jerry and I touch base every few months. In his last e-mail he wrote, "The direction that I'd like to take with my new career is becoming clearer and more authentic to me, the more I sit with it. There is a spiritual connection throughout this process that is becoming clearer and more powerful as I move through it; it feels right. How cool is that?"

This is just the beginning

When most people tell me they want to embark on this journey of changing careers, they say it is to "figure out what I want to be when I grow up" or "find the right place for the next 15 years." But this process has not been about "getting it right." Nor has this been about making sure you're set for life from this point on.

You have been working to create a career that fits your life and who you are. You've been discovering yourself and noticing what is emerging outside in the world. Having done these steps, yes, you will feel more at ease and confident.

But you will change. And the world will change. What makes you valuable in the eyes of the world and happy inside yourself will depend on you and your ability to keep noticing what arises in you and outside in the world. It will continue to be up to you to do something about that. As the writer Michael DeFreitas said, "Happiness is not something you can afford to entrust to others."

Will, the construction guy who became an advertising executive, told me, "This is not my last career. It's just the next place to park for a while. I'm still evolving."

> *"There are enough ways in this world for everyone to have a path of their own."*
>
> Somebody's mother said this; heard on a radio interview in 1997

In fact, he is indeed working on his next career, which incorporates his most joyful skills, knowledge, experience he's gained in advertising, and what he cares about deeply: changing the world for the better. He's looking to do that by telling stories—something he realized he was skilled at when he stood up at those City Council and community meetings years ago. Only this time, he is telling stories by writing screenplays that he hopes to turn into movies.

You might stay with this next career. And again, you may decide to change or adapt it somehow to a new direction. You don't need to reinvent yourself, as so many people tell me they need to do. Just *be* yourself. When legendary rock-and-roller Rod Stewart came out with his collection of classic ballads, he talked about the new direction his career was taking. He advised others to "Just do what you want to do, be yourself and you'll knock people out."

From this point on, look at yourself as a calculated risk taker. This is a powerful way to make it safer to take risks, said James Citrin and Richard Smith, authors of *The 5 Patterns of Extraordinary Careers*.

So, for example, instead of seeing your new career and possible changes after that as part of a plan, call it an experiment. This is safer, because experiments prove or disprove a hypothesis. Plans are riskier because they're either met or not met. You can adjust what you learn from an experiment and cycle that back into your thinking.

The company eBay applies this experimental approach to product development. They test out new ideas on their customers by getting feedback and then adapt based on that input. They put new features on the site, get more feedback and adapt again.

Apply this thinking to your career. See your next career—and others that may follow—as an experiment based on the best information you have at the time and what you think you want. Make the best choice you can and see what you learn from the experiment. Then cycle that into your thinking, so that over time, you're open to the changes that can lead you to the next best thing.

Most of all, continue to build upon the gifts you have been graced with. So when the time comes that you look back and ask, "What have I done with my days?" you can say, "Everything I wanted."

Acknowledgments

Umpteen people helped me make this book possible and I am grateful to all of them.

For the people I know who introduced me to people I now know, I thank Mary Beth Crocker, Sue McDonald, Sarah Stahr, Barry Gibberman, Adam Cannon, Dr. Paul DeLeeuw, Dr. Eddie Saeks and Karen Saeks.

I thank the seekers of something better who openly shared their stories and are some of the most dedicated and hard-working souls I know: Joe Barker, Beth Soon, Beth Planzer, Dr. Joseph DeLeeuw, Gary Dick, Joel Saeks, Charles Duus, Morry Rosenthal, Leonard Hollander, Ed Weinsberg, Russell Alexander, Pat Sayre, Jason Brown, Merritt Mitchell, Jude Schneider, Aliza Sherman Risdahl, Linda Furiate and Lisa Dennerll.

For the wise words they generously shared or information I wouldn't have known about otherwise, I thank Rabbi Norman Cohen, Dr. Eric Eiselt, Don Hauptman, Rick Krawczeski, Brenda McSwigan, Duane Peters, Kate Pocock, Allison Nadelhaft, Wayne Pinnell, Bruce Cox, Jane Stout, Emily Carlton, Rosemary Deitzer, Adam Steinharter, Nick Powills, Scott Rodgers, Michael Wayne, Kim Falcone, Jeff Cornish, Kelley McKeon and Rowena Frith.

I am especially appreciative to Randy McNutt, who read my manuscript and pointed out things that somehow just get right past you.

I thank the people who gave me the opportunity to talk to others about their careers: Craig Schwed, Dave Mason, Annette Meurer and Amy Brock.

For readers of my column who have written me from California, New York, New Jersey, Florida, Michigan, Ohio, Hawaii, Illinois, Indiana, Tennessee, South Carolina, Washington, Texas, everywhere in between, and across the world.

For their guidance and support that helped me do this project and everything else in the meantime: Joni Demmel, my mother and father, my agent Andrea Pedolsky, my editor Marisa Bulzone, Dennis Rutherford, Steve Gillen and Kelly Mott.

My sincere thanks to Anne Kostick, who believed in my idea in the first place.

For their sage words that inspire me daily, Ralph Waldo Emerson and Willem de Kooning.

And enormous appreciation to my husband, Greg Newberry, who, although he has enough to do in his life, read every word and, as always, had insightful stories to share.

Index

N

Nag buddy, 244–45
Negative information, avoiding, 206–7
Networking, 191–94
Noe, John R., 248–49, 250

O

Older career changers:
   advantages of, 221
   issues, concerns, and fears of, 163–65,
      167–68
   second careers after retirement and,
      17–18
Online research, 109–12
   example of, 110–12
   online conversations in, 138–39
   sources for, 111
   on target companies and people, 191
Organizations:
   culture of. See Culture of organization
   research conclusions and, 118–19
   targeting, 191
   values of, 64
   working environment of. See
      Environment at work

P

Pasteur, Louis, 247
Pastry chefs, demand for, 115–17
"Path with heart," Castaneda on, 99
People:
   explaining career change to, 206–8
   getting attention of, 197–203
   getting information from, 106, 109–10,
      133–39, 161, 191–92
   getting insight into yourself from, 66–67
   holding attention of, 203–6. See also
      Stump speech
   supportive, 247
   targeting, in process of finding new posi-
      tion, 191–94
   unplanned interactions with, 201–2
   worrying about opinions of, 163–69
People with whom you work:
   avoiding negative information about,
      206–7
   in Career Objective, 69, 82, 102
   matching up job offers with, 239
   naming what you like about, 61–62
   research conclusions and, 119, 122, 123
Performance reviews, 66

Personal financial advisers, demand for,
   116
Pet industry, trends in, 127
Phone calls, to people you're targeting,
   198–200
Physical ailment or disability, career change
   related to, 16–17, 19
Physicians, potential careers of, 13
Pinnell, Wayne, 115
Pitts, Soni, 148
Plans:
   breaking into doable tasks, 183
   mapping out, 181–88
   short-term, 188
Politics, 140–41
   example of online search on, 110
   thinking about career in, 107
Popcorn, Faith, 149
Post-secondary education administrators,
   demand for, 116
Project management, trends in, 131–32
Promotions managers, demand for, 116
Psychology, as category of life, 92
Public health, as category of life, 88

Q

Quality of life:
   defining criteria for, 71–72
   dissatisfaction with, 19, 44
   matching up job offers with, 238
   survey of women's views on, 73

R

Realism:
   about career options, 184
   idealistic, 182
Reality, confronting, 133, 159
Recruiters, 235
Reeve, Christopher, 180
Regulations, new, potential jobs and, 108
Relaxed Wanderer (tea recipe), 33
Relevance, likeability and, 214, 215
Repeating mistakes, avoiding, 36
Repplier, Agnes, 253
Research, 106–51
   in confronting and managing issues,
      concerns, and fears, 159
   in determining if you'll like new career,
      161
   drawing appropriate conclusions from,
      117–20, 139–43

Y